D0537385

NOBODY HERE BUT US
PIONEERS OF THE NORTH

Illustrations by Fred Forster

Nobody Here But Us

Pioneers of the North

Moira Farrow

J.J. DOUGLAS LTD. VANCOUVER 1975

Canadian Shared Cataloguing in Publication Data

Farrow, Moira.
    Nobody here but us: pioneers of the North

    1. Northwest, Canadian — Biography. 2.
Frontier and pioneer life — Northwest, Can-
adian. I. Title.
F   920'.0711'1
⌈LC: F1060.3.F37⌉
ISBN 0-88894-087-4

Library of Congress catalog card number:
75-24547

75 76 77 78 79 5 4 3 2 1

J.J. DOUGLAS LTD.
1875 Welch Street
North Vancouver, British Columbia

Map Craig Ainscough
Design Nancy Legue
Jacket design Fred Forster
Typesetting Domino-Link Word & Data Processing Ltd.
Printed and bound in Canada Hunter Rose Company

This book
could not have been written
without financial help from
the Canada Council
and leave of absence from
the Vancouver Sun.
I gratefully acknowledge
this assistance
and co-operation.

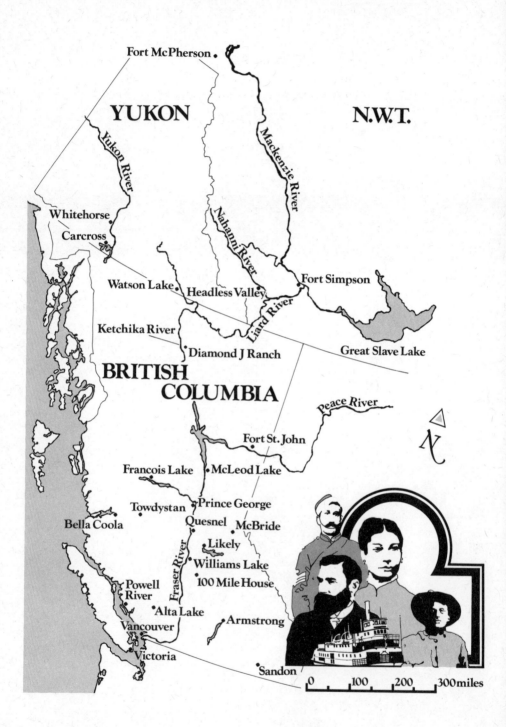

Fort McPherson

YUKON

N.W.T.

Yukon River

Mackenzie River

Whitehorse

Carcross

Nahanni River

Watson Lake   Headless Valley

Fort Simpson

Liard River

Ketchika River

Great Slave Lake

Diamond J Ranch

BRITISH
COLUMBIA

Peace River

Fort St. John

Francois Lake   McLeod Lake

Towdystan   Prince George

Bella Coola

Quesnel   McBride

Likely

Fraser River

Williams Lake

100 Mile House

Powell
River

Alta Lake

Vancouver

Armstrong

Victoria

Sandon

0   100   200   300 miles

Contents

Introduction

It all started with Skook Davidson—the crusty old rancher whose wild adventures and love of horses were talked about far beyond the borders of British Columbia. His later years were lonely—his health and wealth sacrificed to his beloved animals.

I had often heard about Skook while traveling around northern B.C. on assignment for the Vancouver *Sun*. But getting to see him was another matter. His isolated ranch could only be reached by chartered float plane. And even if one arrived, there was no guarantee that Skook would be in the mood for a chat. His short temper and colorful vocabulary were well known to anyone within range of his radio telephone.

Attempting to arrange an appointment with him was, I was told, an exercise in futility. "Go and try your luck" was the advice I was given.

So one lucky day, my plane touched down on the choppy waters of the Kechika River while Skook sat in his wagon on the bank scowling at his unexpected visitor. "If I'd known you were coming, woman, I'd have shaved," were his opening words. From then on, my problems were over. He talked so much that I ran out of space in my notebook.

The story about Skook in the *Sun* drew more mail than I had ever received before in many years of journalism.

It was astonishing how many people had met or heard of the old rancher even though he lived miles from any road or town. And everyone who responded to the story seemed delighted that Skook's amazing life had been recorded in some way, however briefly. Even people who had never met him said they enjoyed reading about his struggle to build a wilderness ranch.

Nearly all had in mind another B.C. character who "would make a great story." The fear was always expressed that unless these pioneer stories were written down soon, they would be lost forever because B.C.'s first generation of settlers was dying off fast.

It seemed to me that there was both the interest and the need to warrant a collection of pioneer stories. The toughest part of the project, I soon discovered, was deciding which people to interview. The possible candidates ran into scores and everyone I talked to suggested more names. The book could easily have become the project of a lifetime and, at times, I thought it would.

I interviewed far more than the dozen people whose stories appear in this book. Many people with fascinating lives had, sadly, become too old to do justice to their recollections. Some had to be eliminated simply because they had lived in a place or worked at a job already represented by another personality in the book. And others were dropped because they had lived too much of their lives outside B.C.

All I can do is apologize to those who have been left out—including those I never even met. There is always another pioneer story around the next bend in the road and if I had kept on going this book would never have been written.

The people described here do not represent a definitive selection of the most colorful pioneer stories in the north. They are merely some of the strong and unusual people who lived in B.C., the Yukon and the Northwest Territories when the first white men began settling the Pacific northwest.

I was constantly surprised, when talking to these pioneers, by the way they stressed the fun they had had in their early years. Most of them had led rugged lives in conditions that, by today's standards, were primitive. Certainly they mentioned the long hours of hard and often boring work they put in. But there was pride in the hardships endured. Apart from the obvious tragedies, like the death of a child, their recollections were full of joy.

They talked much of the friendliness of the early communities, the good-neighbor response to any form of trouble, the pleasure of making one's own entertainment, and the abundance of good, cheap food such as game and home-grown vegetables.

It was almost impossible to find a woman who had led an individually remarkable life, because sixty-odd years ago, women in this part of the word were still Victorians. They worked as hard and as long as the men, but they accepted the housewife role without question. And this is scarcely surprising because, as they often recalled, their working day was from sunrise to sunset. Time to sit down and read a book, let alone contemplate their role in society, was an almost unheard of luxury.

The most engaging characteristic of these pioneers was their frankness. They had no interest in keeping up with the Joneses, then or now, and they had no hesitation in expressing their opinions.

For instance, they spoke freely about their relationships with their Indian neighbors, and opinions differed enormously. Some heaped praise on the Indians, others were blunt in their animosity. And in many hours of conversation about B.C.'s wildlife, not one person agreed with the current game management policy of protecting wolves. These pioneers had a fierce hatred of wolves that would horrify a wildlife biologist today. The fact that their opinions did not conform to current thinking did not bother them at all.

I learned in my travels that northern hospitality and pioneer cooking are alive and well. From blueberry pie in McBride to homemade bread in Fort Simpson, I was welcomed with good food and great kindliness.

I also learned never to expect these old-timers to be dozing in a rocking chair. One man could not speak with me right away, because he was hunched over a broadcast hockey game in his one-room cabin; one, aged 100, was away on a mining trip in the bush; another dumped the manuscript of his autobiography in a cardboard box at my feet, and yet another was busy hauling a cast iron stove several miles through the bush.

Many encounters along the way were unforgettable. There were, for instance the helicopter crew who let me hitchhike a ride from the Northwest Territories to B.C, the float plane pilot who practically stood his aircraft on its nose so that I could see a grizzly bear and her cubs, and the Yukon bus driver freighting a juke box and sack of potatoes who told me he had cried with happiness when he got his haulage licence.

To all these people, those who talked and those who helped, I am deeply grateful.

The name Canada is alleged to have come from a Spanish or Portuguese phrase meaning "nobody here." That's what the early explorers wrote across their map in the blank space that was Canada. But they were wrong. The Indians had lived here for centuries. And as the nineteenth century began, the trickle of white settlers turned into a torrent. Soon there was "nobody here"—but us.

Moira Farrow
1975

Chapter 1
"Skook"
Guide, Packer, Horse Rancher

Skook Davidson's name is legend in northern British Columbia and so many stories are told about him that it is hard to sift fact from fiction. But undoubtedly Skook was the greatest horseman B.C. has ever seen or is likely to see. His passion for horses was his reason for living, and it explains why he never married and had children. And for years it kept him from the comforts of civilization when he became old and crippled.

Skook was also famous throughout the north for his hell-raising, his hard drinking, his quick wit, his enormous generosity, and his ability to survive—often alone—in a rugged, lonely land, which most men could tolerate for only a few months at a time. His nickname of Skook came from the Indian word "skookum" meaning strong, and he lived up to it.

From 1939 until he was driven out by a fire and broken health in 1972, Skook reigned as the laird of the Kechika. His Diamond J Ranch at the northern end of the Rocky Mountain trench was located in the wide Kechika River valley, about a hundred air miles south of Watson Lake, Yukon Territory. The ranch had no road connection with the outside world, so river boat or aircraft provided the only access to Skook and his 200 horses.

The ranch, at the foot of 6,267-foot Terminus Mountain, had half a dozen log buildings and corrals, hundreds of miles of trail, and hunting rights believed to cover more than five thousand square miles. His territory was originally much larger, but he sold or gave away thousands of square miles to a friend on the other side of the valley.

"I never wanted to be rich—as long as I can square up, I say to hell with it," was Skook's financial philosophy.

John Ogilvie Davidson—to give Skook his full name—was born in Scotland in a small village near Aberdeen in 1892. He often lied about his age, and that year is as close to the truth as anyone is ever likely to get.

His father was a gardener with ten children, so life was far from soft for the Davidson family. But it was too tame for young Skook, whose thirst for adventure was keen. One day, the restless boy read a story about gold mining in the Cariboo and made up his mind to try it himself.

Skook was thirteen or fourteen when he landed in Halifax and traveled across the country to British Columbia. He only had about $10 in his pocket when he arrived in Ashcroft, and he still had it days later, after walking and hitching wagon rides to 150 Mile House, because no one would take money from such a youngster. Skook was so ignorant about horses then that he had to be shown how to put on a harness. He worked on the boats on the Fraser

River, spent some time as a ranch hand in Soda Creek, and drove teams of horses for railroad construction contractors. "Each horse weighed a ton and ate a bag of oats a day," he said.

In the Hazelton area, Skook met the famous old packer Cataline and worked with him for a while. But Skook was always a horseman and was never very interested in the mules used most of the time by Cataline.

However, he did take a fancy to a pretty Indian girl who was Cataline's companion. The packer was getting to be an old man and he did not take kindly to his girl being eyed by the tough young Scotsman. So Cataline dealt with this unfair competition by threatening Skook with a knife so vigorously that he left red marks, which were visible for days, on Skook's throat. "After that, the girl would wiggle right past me and I never even saw her," said Skook, grinning.

Eventually, he saved enough money to buy his own eight-horse team and started freighting all over the interior. But after war was declared, he did not stay out of the action for long. In 1915, he drove his team and wagon to Ashcroft, sold them, and joined up.

Skook's war record was magnificent. He won the Distinguished Conduct Medal with two bars, the Military Medal, and the Croix de Guerre for bravery in several famous battles including the Somme and Passchendaele.

After the war, he returned to B.C. and his beloved horses. In the 1920s, Skook made his living by running pack horse trains for government surveys, and he crisscrossed the province visiting communities as far flung as Telegraph Creek, Bella Coola and Fort St. James. Life was never dull in spite of the many miles of trail to be covered every day. There was the bar at Telegraph Creek that seldom closed, and the Swedish store keeper at Bella Coola who wanted Skook to marry one of his pretty blonde daughters. But, as usual, Skook ducked and ran whenever the prospect of matrimony came too close.

In the 1930s, Skook freighted for Bob and Bert McCorkell, who operated placer mines at Manson Creek and Germansen River, using teams of horses, wagons and sleighs on the pack trail between Fort St. James and Germansen Landing.

"Skook liked his horses and they came first," said Ron Campbell of Vanderhoof, who freighted with Skook during some of his years with McCorkell. "He bought a trap line in Dome Creek and trapped out of there in the winter and then packed for McCorkell in the summer. That was Skook's life."

Campbell earned $15 a month when he started working with the pack train in the 1930s. He was the bell boy, which meant he led the mare wearing a bell and the rest of the horses followed behind. "At that time, thirty dollars a month was top wages, so for a kid of thirteen that fifteen dollars a month was pretty good, but I had to do the cooking too," said Campbell.

"The freight charges were ten or twelve cents a pound when we had pack horses and I remember we had a three hundred-pound cookstove on one horse. The freight war was a running battle—the freighters were at each other's throats over prices."

By 1936, trucks could make it into Manson Creek and eventually, all the freighters had to switch from horses to machinery. Skook ended up with a tractor and did not enjoy it.

In 1939, the Second World War split up the freighting crews, and Skook found a job with the provincial government running a pack train for survey crews. He decided to spend the winter in the Kechika valley because, on a previous occasion, he had found it a good place to winter horses.

Skook came into the Kechika in 1939, alone. His only companions were his horses and a two-way radio, the first in the valley. "I think it was around November first when I came in and I never saw a damn soul until March," he said.

"I was never lonely—I worked too hard. When you're alone, there's nothing to do but work. People used to ask me what I was doing in this god-forsaken country, but later on they all wanted to come in."

That first winter the only food Skook took in with him was twenty-five pounds of flour, ten pounds of sugar, and one pound each of tea and coffee. The following winter a man named Johnny Rasmussen joined him and butter was added to the shopping list, an extravagance of which Skook thoroughly disapproved. But game was plentiful and the men never went short of meat.

And so the Diamond J Ranch was established. The name Diamond probably came from the diamond hitch always used by packers and the J from Skook's first name, John. The first thing Skook built was a cabin and later a barn, corrals, many outbuildings, and miles of fencing were added.

That was how Skook and the Kechika valley became inseparable for more than thirty years. He loved the place—even though, as he got older, the rugged winters with temperatures of sixty below for several days on end were very hard on his health. The climate was semi-arid with a comparatively light snowfall for such a northern area, and that made it easier on the horses than some other areas in the same latitude. However, in winters when the wind was fierce and blew the snow into drifts, horses had a rough time even in this valley, and many died.

In the Kechika, Skook was securely isolated from the noise and traffic of civilization. Various people came to the ranch to work with or for Skook for a while and then left again. He was always a permanent fixture. At first, all supplies had to be packed into the ranch from Fort Ware, a round trip of 200 miles. Skook packed everything from a canoe to a bathtub along the Fort Ware trail that borders the Kechika and Fox rivers and runs over the 4,000-foot Sifton Pass.

In later years, all Skook's gear came in by plane—

usually a float plane that landed on the Kechika, a fast-flowing river that looks shallow but is quite deep. Locals sometimes call it the Muddy River. Planes with wheels or skis—and very brave pilots—sometimes landed in Skook's hay meadow and that was an experience never forgotten by anyone who tried it.

Skook's reputation as a packer was first class. He really knew the business and was always in demand. He left on his packing trips in May and didn't get back to the ranch until the end of October or early November. According to Rudy Pop, who also had a pack train in the Kechika country at one time and eventually became a well-known Vancouver furrier, Skook sometimes traveled up to five hundred miles on one trip. His pack trains were often a mile long, because some of the horses had their foals along to learn how to pack.

"Once I met up with Skook at a lake in the Kechika country and he named it after me—Pop Lake—and it's still called that today," said Pop. "Skook liked naming things— he was always naming horses after his friends. He said to me once, 'It's easy to give them a horse because they can never take it out of here.'" Eventually, there were scores of horses in the Kechika valley which belonged, theoretically, to Skook's friends and their children.

In the 1940s, Skook was given the rank of special constable in the B.C. police force because his knowledge of the north was a great help to the police in some of their more remote cases. He arrested a murder suspect at Fort Ware in March 1943 and kept him until the police managed to fly in to the lonely, snowbound outpost. The murder victim, who happened to be the suspect's wife, was exhumed immediately and a post mortem conducted on the frozen body. Then it was the job of the magistrate, the doctor, the police sergeant and Skook to rebury the body.

Around midnight, when the burial party straightened up from their labors in the moonlight, Skook broke the icy silence with the words, "Let's give her a soldier's farewell." He drew his gun and solemnly fired six shots in the air. Then the sergeant produced a mickey of rum and it was wordlessly passed from hand to hand to restore the gravediggers' circulation. When the dead woman was laid to rest, the men turned to Skook to say a few last words. "Well," he said thoughtfully, after a short pause, "I'm damn glad it was her and not me."

In 1942, Skook was the packer for the U.S.-sponsored survey of a railway route between Prince George and Alaska. The survey was completed, but the railway was never built because the threat of invasion by Japan faded in 1943.

"I was with the U.S. Engineering Department in one of the survey parties and I first met Skook at Fort Ware," recalled George Fey. "Skook watched us unloading our gear and all the boxes had USED stamped on the sides. I remember the first thing he said to us was, 'What's the matter, can't you afford new stuff?' Of course, USED were the initials of the engineering department."

Although Fey knew Skook personally for only a few months of the summer of 1942, he corresponded with him for about thirty years afterward. "I admired Skook—I'd have liked to lead the kind of life he did, but I couldn't," said Fey, explaining why he kept in contact with Skook. "He was a true Scotsman—he saved his pennies and spent his dollars. Twice when we were out on the survey, he brought in a couple of cases of liquor and threw a big party for us, way up there in the sticks." According to Fey, Skook drank 151-proof Demerara rum because he did not think Scotch "had any kick to it."

Whenever Skook left the ranch, to go south to Prince George or north to Lower Post, the action surrounding him sparked stories that spread for miles and survived for years. Skook was tough, noisy and hard-boiled, but he had his own rigid code of ethics. Part of this code was that he never took advantage of the Indian women of the north, as so many white men did at that time.

"Whenever he finished up a survey trip, he'd generally go to Prince George with the whole crew and they'd have a big party that lasted for a month or two, or however long their money held out," said Fey. "During one of these parties, Skook decided to marry an old girl friend he had known years back in Winnipeg. So he got the gang together, chartered a plane, and flew back there, only to find she'd been married for years and had a family. But that didn't stop Skook. He went back up to his hotel and had a reception anyway—even though there wasn't a bride."

Every fall, Skook descended on Lower Post like a hurricane, slapped down about a thousand dollars on the hotel bar, and announced that everyone in town was to have a drink on him. And they did. The whole community turned out for a two-day party and drank until Skook's money was gone.

"But that was his hobby, his way of life, and he enjoyed it," said the Yukon big-game guide Johnnie Johns, who took part in many of Skook's parties.

Two young American women who watched Skook's antics one night in a bar in Watson Lake will not forget the experience. Skook, wearing his usual black stetson and surrounded by his gang of cowboys, was like a character out of a western movie and his stories grew more colorful as the evening progressed. Suddenly, he leaped out of his chair, ripped a bear skin off the bar wall, and presented it to one of the girls with the words, "There you are, honey, I always told you I'd give you furs."

One of the many women Skook was interested in, but never got around to marrying, lived in Prince George. On this occasion, so the story goes, Skook did propose, but the woman said she would only consider the idea when Skook had $1,000 in the bank. So he worked hard, put $1,000 in the bank, and went back to town to claim her. She went back on her word and raised her price to $2,000. The next time Skook returned to Prince George he had the necessary $2,000, but he did not go near the woman. Finally, she could stand his silence no longer and told him she was ready to get married. "Well," said Skook, "I ain't." And that was the end of that romance.

For all Skook's well-known spending sprees, he also carried out many quiet acts of generosity and kindness. Over the years, he helped all kinds of people, from the author Rich Hobson (who was short of groceries one year until Skook stepped in) to young Indians who needed some horses to set themselves up in business.

Skook's great love of horses and his skill at breeding them were well known. His horses were never in-bred, and most of them died naturally of old age, because he "pensioned them off" when they were past working. "Hell on the horses and the woodpile," was Skook's favorite expression when the temperature dropped to fifty below.

The government kept a lot of horses in northern B.C. for survey work and Skook was paid to look after them in the winter. This led, inevitably, to confusion over ownership of some of the animals, and Skook had many arguments with the government. What Skook failed to mention in these disputes was that some of the horses branded Diamond J had originally carried a government brand. As a former police constable, Skook got a kick out of re-branding stolen horses.

The survey and construction of the 1,500-mile Alaska Highway from 1942 to 1943 was another major project with which Skook was involved, supplying horses and packing for the work crews. And when the highway was built it came, at Lower Post, to within about 150 miles of the Diamond J's home ranch. Compared with the isolation of the past, that meant the ranch was practically in touch with civilization.

As government survey work in northern B.C. came to an end, Skook found he was doing a lot of packing for mining companies. Then came the day, some time in the late 1940s, that Skook had to take out his first hunting party. He never liked hunting and he only turned to it as a last resort to pay his bills.

As Skook put it in a letter: "The hunting party game I'm in now is lots of work and a short season, but it pays the bills. My hunters come from the U.S., mainly Texas. Hunters are all brags, they always want a bigger head every year." He left the hunters in no doubt about his feelings, if any of them became greedy. He once grabbed the rifle out of Rudy Pop's hand and jammed it into the mud because he thought Pop had done enough shooting.

Skook took out only four or five hunting parties every season, compared to his nearest neighbor who took out up to forty. That sort of hunting, which cleaned the country right out of game, disgusted Skook. He never hunted the same area more than one year out of three, a technique he could indulge in because he had such an enormous territory. Consequently, vast areas were left untouched by hunters for several years at a time and became very rich in game.

Taking out so few hunters always meant that Skook ran the risk of financial disaster. If one hunting party cancelled at the last moment, leaving Skook with a full crew he had to pay, there was little he could do to recoup the loss. This sort of problem occurred quite often.

Skook's ranch never went in for comfort. The dirt-roofed cabins leaked in heavy rain and the plumbing was nonexistent. In later days, a bath-house and washing machine were added to give a semblance of modern conveniences, but it was always a spartan place. However, that did not bother the hunters who came from thousands of miles away to Skook's territory because his reserves of game were among the finest in North America. To the hunters, that was all that mattered. Skook's territory had everything from grizzly bear to Stone sheep.

A hunting trip with Skook sometimes covered up to three hundred miles and lasted for several weeks. The unusual people who came to hunt with Skook ranged from rich Chicago gangsters to the brother of the Shah of Iran, Prince Abdorreza.

"Skook treated him as a real person for the first time in his life," related John Anderson." Skook would holler at him the same as he did to everyone else. One day, when the prince couldn't find a suitable place to go to the toilet, Skook yelled, 'Jesus Christ, go and straddle yourself a small spruce tree—how the hell do you think I got to walk like this?' "

The day the prince left, he produced from his baggage a silver bowl and tray, intended as a gift to the governor of Texas. He presented them to Skook instead. Said the prince: "I've heard of men like you, but this is the first time I've met one." Skook was very proud of his silverware, but he never knew what to do with it. He said the plate and tray were too shallow for baking in and not even much use as feeding bowls for the cats and dogs.

During the hunting season Skook employed about twenty guides, mostly Indians, and a cook who had to be good to keep the hunters happy. Skook himself loathed cooking. He once made hot cakes with sourdough batter that had such a greenish tinge his hunters became sick just looking at it. And he was known to have dined off a can of peaches and a can of sardines, mixed together. "That's a bloody fact—they weren't too bad," he said.

From 1939 until a few months after the fire of 1972, Skook kept a diary and made entries almost every day. Most of these diaries, scrawled in pencil or pen in battered old notebooks, were lost in the blaze. They recorded a tough, lonely life that was devoted to horses and a constant battle against the elements.

For years, Skook was the only white man in the Kechika valley. He frequently employed Indians to work on the ranch, bought furs from them, and hired them to guide his hunters. He knew many of these men for decades and they were constantly in and out of his cabin, but his relationship with his Indian neighbors, according to his writings, was always cool and critical.

Again and again he noted in his diary that certain Indians had come over "to put the bite on me as usual." Occasionally, he did not let them into the cabin, but usually he handed over the groceries that were requested, such as "25 pounds of flour, 10 pounds of sugar, one pound of tea and one pound of lard."

Presumably, the Indians repaid Skook for the groceries by working around the ranch, but the diaries make far more mention of food being handed out than they do about work. Every year he paid off his Indian guides with over a thousand dollars each and they left immediately to get drunk in Lower Post or Watson Lake. Skook, forgetting his own wild drunks before his arthritis forced him to quit drinking, was intolerant of this behavior. "They'll be back in two weeks, broke, sick and sorry," he said.

There was one Indian who won Skook's unstinted admiration, a woman called Mabel Frank. For years, she worked as a cook for Skook's hunting parties and was a great help to him. She was a wonderful cook and a very pleasant person.

Skook's most frequent companion in the Kechika valley was a white man named Willard Freer, who had also been a packer. For years, Freer lived with Skook as a sort of partner or chief wrangler. The two men had a difference of opinion around 1959 after which Freer built a cabin and opened a trading post about fourteen miles down the valley from the Diamond J. The dispute could not have been serious, because Skook gave Freer enough horses to set himself up as an independent packer.

Hugh Gabrielse of the Geological Survey of Canada, who knew Skook well in the 1950s, said Skook was already a legend when he first met him. Gabrielse recounted some stories he had heard of Skook's early packing expeditions. Some were almost starvation trips because they ran out of food before getting home. Even Skook admitted that on occasion, he had been reduced to eating raw meat.

"A fellow by the name of Pat Cooke often went on

long trips with Skook and, as Pat told it, he would literally fall off his horse when they got to camp," said Gabrielse. "Skook would always see that the horses were fixed up first and then he'd get together what little food they had. Pat got so weak he'd lean up against a tree as Skook was saddling the horses. Pat liked to joke that eventually he got so weak he couldn't even cough."

The pack trains had to make a very difficult crossing of the Finlay River at Fort Ware where the current is extremely fast. Skook did it many times, but once he was swept off his horse and vanished. Everyone assumed the worst. Then, out of the water onto the beach strode Skook's horse, and hanging onto its tail was the man himself.

"They turned him over, poured out the water and as far as Skook was concerned it was nothing more than a soaking," said Gabrielse. "But living that kind of life in that country meant that Skook probably had similar experiences several times a year. To most people they would be hair raising, but he just shrugged them off as part of life. And he also had some very rough accidents. He was run over by a wagon once, and another time his horse jammed him up against a corral and he broke two ribs.

"Most of the great stories about him come from a time when he was drinking. You see, he would only hit Lower Post and Watson Lake once or twice a year and then he'd really hang one on, but for the rest of the year he probably drank very little.

"He enjoyed having a visitor for a few hours, for half a day, whenever it was possible for anyone to drop in, but longer than that and he'd had enough. Often a man living all on his own gets very parochial in his outlook, but Skook was quite a philosophical type. Whenever we visited him he obviously loved to have someone around for a while to air his views on, but after half a day or more he suddenly could not get along with a person any longer. I realized this was the case, so I made myself scarce after a certain length of time and I never had any spats with him."

Skook Davidson

Gabrielse was a witness to Skook's passion for all animals. He was a conservationist through and through and he voiced his disgust at people who overhunted, in terms that were brutally blunt. "Skook's great hope was that when he left the country, part of it would be set aside as a wildlife preserve," said Gabrielse. However, that wish never came true because Skook's hunting territory was taken over, and attempts to make the Kechika valley into a park came to nothing.

Wolves were the only animals Skook detested. He spent much of his ranching life locked in a fierce struggle with the game department (now the fish and wildlife branch) over his desire to poison off as many wolves as possible.

Skook had a theory that it was the large amount of lime in the Kechika country that made the Stone sheep there grow such large heads. He was fascinated by the way the sheep used to butt their heads together, making a booming sound that echoed through the hills. "I couldn't figure out when I was first in here what the awful booming sound was," he said.

Skook had opinions about every animal in his territory. The grizzlies thrived, he believed, because of the plentiful supply of salmon in the rivers, and the eagles were numerous because they could feed on the lambs. "I've seen an eagle knock a lamb into a canyon and then dive down and get it," he said.

Most biologists are convinced that wolves kill only old, weak or sick animals and will never attack a strong and healthy specimen.

"That bunch in the game department in Victoria say the wolves won't hurt the game," said Skook in a letter to a friend. "The damn fools—but you can't tell them anything. They think they know lots because they went to school lots and we have not. They get what they know out of books, but we have lived in the bush all our lives and see the kill the wolves pull off on the game. I'm sure fed up about it."

In his diary and letters, Skook wrote endlessly about his war with the wolves. Mainly he complained that the game department would not let him put out poison—but he sometimes put it out all the same.

"The wolves have cleaned the valley of moose," he wrote in 1965. "Not a damn one left and all the deer are gone. The sheep and goats are above timber line, too scared to come down, and there's no feed for them up there. I talked to some of the biologists at the guides' meeting in Fort St. John, but they just laughed at me and said the wolves only killed old stuff. But I know they always kill the calves first and I've never seen them kill an old one."

Wolves were not the only subject on which he disagreed with the game department officers. He often claimed that they ordered him to hunt far more than he would have liked. "If we keep on taking out this much game it's going to be hard to get game in a few years, but the people in charge don't seem to know this," he wrote. "They are after the dollar and don't give a damn as long as they get it."

The first kind word Skook ever had for wildlife officials was when they told him his was the only outfit "which the hunters had not written to them kicking about." Skook savored that compliment because he knew he was never easy on his hunters. It was early to bed and early to rise at the Diamond J and the quality of the meals was unpredictable.

Much of Skook's time was spent bellowing and cussing into his radio set. By radio, he arranged for men and freight to fly in and out and he hired most of his staff without seeing them.

Quick temper and swear words were only one part of Skook's character. He loved to joke, to tease his cowboys, and to mimic everyone who crossed his path. Sometimes he would give his cowboys what he called a Diamond J haircut before they went into town, which meant that he practically scalped them. "That's how you can tell if a girl loves you. If

she likes you with no damn hair, she'll like you with hair—
get me?" said Skook as he wielded the clippers. "You don't
need no hair cut for quite a while after a Diamond J cut."

Skook had all kinds of unusual expressions dating
from his varied experiences. A few French words like
"comprenez," which he had picked up during the war, and
some Indian phrases he had learned from his cowboys were
scattered through his conversation. The phrase he liked
best was "you lazy mavericks," and he directed it at five
minute intervals at man or beast.

"The Maverick" was also the title of a poem that
Skook loved to quote because it summed up his philosophy
of life. It is impossible to say where he found the poem, but
it goes:

> I believe that all my lifetime
> It has never been my norm
> To be counted with those people
> Who forever must conform.
> I have at times a creature been
> Who has traveled far away,
> When hard and fast tradition
> Said you simply had to stay.
> And I also have not listened
> When conformity would preach
> That to climb the social ladder
> Self control you had to reach.
> I likewise have not followed
> In the footsteps of the crowd,
> And would only smile on others
> When it came to cheer out loud.
> But I think that all us humans
> On occasions get a kick
> When balking and revolting
> We become the maverick.

Much of the flying in and out to Diamond J was done by another famous man of the north, George Dalziel. When Skook first knew him, Dalziel was one of the north's great pioneer flyers, renowned for his daredevil exploits. During the 1930s he flew one of the few aircraft that existed in northern Canada, and was known as Canada's only flying fur trapper. Skook greatly admired Dalziel's skill as a pilot: he could throw a package out of his plane so accurately that it would land nearly at the feet of the man he was aiming at.

As Skook grew older, his concern for his horses became almost an obsession. Each animal was an individual to him; at a glance, he could reel off each horse's name, its age, the month it was born, and several anecdotes about its life. He could do this for every one of his 200 horses. Any man who dared make a critical comment about any of Skook's horses soon wished he had not.

He flew in tons of oats to feed his horses in winter, sometimes as many as ten tons. In 1969, it cost him $1,000 a month to air lift supplies of oats. "It costs like hell, but it's better than having a bunch of dead horses in the spring," said Skook. "So far, I have had four head die. They were old horses, but it sure hurts me to see them lie down and die, because I knew them so long."

The skeletons of long-dead horses along the trails around the ranch made Skook nostalgic. "Goldarn it, she was a good one, too," he said, looking down at a pile of bleached bones. "That's Belle—she was thirty years old," as he pointed to what seemed to be a rib cage under a tree.

Skook's affection for animals included cats and dogs, as well as horses. He constantly cursed his dogs—"Get out of there, you knotheads" was a favorite expression. But he was very proud of the way they and his four or five cats followed him around all the time.

This is how Skook, in a letter to a friend, described the death of his cat Tom, in 1968: "When I got back from the river and put the team away he was still lying on the bed. I picked him up and petted him and he tried to lick my hand, but died soon after that. He was in pain when he died. I dug a place and put him in a box and the old fellow is out there with a few more of his old friends. I sure miss him and so does the little cat that is left. She looked all over the place for him and follows me all over even in the cold weather."

Skook's compassion for animals in pain was intensified by his own suffering from arthritis. At first, he thought it was rheumatism that made his hips hurt, but he finally learned the truth when he was X-rayed at a hospital in Cassiar. From the early 1960s onward, Skook was in almost constant pain, and friends in the medical profession tried to help by sending him any and every pill they thought would relieve him. But very little did.

In spite of arthritis, Skook continued to ride when most people would have given up all thought of the idea. He climbed into the saddle by mounting from a tree stump beside which his faithful horse Poison stood quietly and as firm as a rock.

The one great joy Skook had in the latter part of his life was his three-week visit to Vancouver in 1964, when he stayed with his old friend, John Anderson.

Anderson had first met Skook in 1956, when he was working for a mining company in the Yukon and needed horses. They became great friends, although they met only occasionally. After Anderson married, his wife Nancy took on the job of corresponding with Skook, although she had not met him. She searched all over Vancouver for the horse medicine he asked her to send him and did not hesitate even when his shopping list included castration clamps. Skook was very grateful for her kindness and reckoned she was "one of the finest girls" he had ever met.

Skook had the time of his life on his first visit to Vancouver in twenty-eight years. Nancy Anderson spoiled him and it was the first time that he had been shown so much kindness. He became devoted to her.

The purpose of the trip was a possible arthritis operation. Skook gave Shaughnessy Hospital no warning of his arrival, but when hospital officials looked at his discharge papers (which he finally found in a back pocket) they admitted him immediately. He threatened the doctors that he would shoot the first one who took off his leg, but he thoroughly enjoyed the pretty nurses who went out of their way to pamper him. The doctors were reluctant to operate because it would have meant a separate operation for each hip and, for Skook, a total of a year flat on his back. Even then, the success of the ordeal was doubtful.

With a patient like Skook, unused to city life and reluctant to leave his ranch for even a week or so "because of the mess" he would return to, the operations would have been hell. The doctors agreed that he had made a wise choice when he decided against hospitalization and they reassured him the pain would go away naturally as his hips stiffened up. But they were wrong. The pain became worse and worse and Skook was in constant misery for years.

Nancy never quite got used to the attention that Skook attracted wherever they went in the city. With his ruddy face, red flannel shirt, levis, metal-studded belt, and white stetson, Skook looked like a movie character, and everyone turned to stare. When he went into a city bank, his unusual appearance made the tellers gape at him in alarm. So, to calm their fears, he bellowed, "Get back to work, girls, I'm not going to hold the place up."

Skook was inclined to be car sick when Nancy drove him around the city, and he explained that this was because the telephone poles went by so fast—much faster than the trees when he was riding a horse.

He packed around with him a bundle of newspaper clippings and photographs which he insisted on showing to everyone he met, in spite of the impatience of some busy professional people. To Skook, it was most important to establish who he was and where he came from before he had a consultation with anyone.

After a session with a chiropodist Skook was

presented with a bill for $15 which he paid without comment. Then, to Nancy's consternation, he announced as he went out of the door, "I could get a squaw in the north to do all that for me and then stay the night with me for nothing."

There was almost a scene in Rudy Pop's elegant fur shop when Nancy took Skook there for a reunion with his old friend. The assistants took one look at Skook and tried to usher him out, but Pop heard the commotion and emerged from the back of the shop. The two men embraced with Skook saying, "You dirty old maverick" while the customers trying on furs stared in astonishment. "You're not riding any more?" asked Pop. "At least I don't have a wooden leg," retorted Skook.

When Nancy took Skook into the pensions office to try to arrange some extra income for him, he nearly wasted all her efforts by insisting that his assets included 200 horses. Nancy had to do some fast talking to make the pensions clerk realize that 200 horses in northern B.C. were scarcely worth anything, because it was too expensive to bring them outside. "Skook's value of things and their real value were two different things," said Nancy.

Skook returned to his ranch in March 1964, after his visit to Vancouver, and found his favorite old saddle horse, Poison, very sick and so lame he could not paw the snow. Poison had always been as gentle as a kitten with Skook, though none of the cowboys could get within twenty feet of him without being kicked. Not long afterward Skook had to shoot Poison to put an end to his suffering and it was a traumatic experience for the old man. Skook wrote in a letter: "We had 17 years on the trails together and it had to end like this. He was going to be pensioned off. No more work this spring. Just let live the rest of his life around the place. It sure hurts me more than anyone will know."

Skook began welcoming the idea of death. His favorite horse was dead and the pain of arthritis never let up. He wrote that he knew he was getting to "the end of the trail," because everything at the ranch seemed to be going wrong.

He considered selling out "if I can get what this damn outfit is worth," but he did no more than talk about it. His painful hips drained all his energy.

"Those damn doctors who said the pain would be over in two years are liars," wrote Skook in 1966. "I guess they meant I would be dead by then."

After his visit to Vancouver, Skook did not leave the ranch for years at a time, except for the odd trip to Watson Lake to get his teeth fixed. "In the old days, I took the pliers and pulled the bad ones out," he said.

He wrote often to the Andersons, recalling that his visit to them was "the finest thing that happened to me for years." He confessed that throughout the visit he had been afraid he might say something "to make you sore at me," because "I'm a damn rough guy and don't know how to talk around girls."

Quite often in these years, as he was so much alone at the ranch, he regretted his lack of family. He wrote and congratulated his friend Jim Sweeney, a West Vancouver dentist who had been kind to him, on the birth of Sweeney's baby. "You have something to work for, Jim, and someone to leave it to when you hit the end of the trail."

When Skook found himself alone now, he did not like it as he once had, because "it gives a guy the damn blues." The last couple of years he spent on the ranch were a nightmare of pain and problems.

By 1971 Skook had given up riding altogether and was complaining that he could hardly walk. Instead, he traveled around the ranch on a horsedrawn wagon from which he climbed down as little as possible. The wagon was not a smooth ride and every jolt was agony for Skook, but at least he was still mobile. The pain was keeping him awake at night and he said he would pay "any price" for pills that would help keep the torment under control. And, on top of the arthritis, his chest hurt in cold weather as a result of an old injury caused by a horse. Then, in April 1972, came a final blow—the suicide of his long-time cook, Mabel Frank.

The shock tipped Skook out of the world of reality and his mind began wandering. It was obvious he could no longer stay at the ranch.

Skook was flown to hospital in Whitehorse in June 1972, then moved to a West Vancouver private hospital. His grasp on reality never returned.

Skook will likely die with his mind still roaming his northern wilderness, and that is the way it should be.

Chapter 2
Johnny Johns
Guide and Trapper

A weather-beaten old moose head is nailed to the front wall of one of the larger log cabins in Carcross, Yukon Territory. A bear skin is thrown over the rail fence. Deer antlers and sheep horns are scattered all over the place. And a tiny grave in the yard is topped with a hand-painted sign, stating that here is buried a well-loved Tahltan bear dog, now gone to a happy hunting ground in the sky.

The cabin is the home of Johnnie Johns, one of the top big game guides in North America until his retirement in 1968. In his private life, he is also a poet, philosopher, comedian, song writer, and leading citizen of Carcross, an an historic community near the British Columbia border.

Johns, a Tagish Indian who was born in the Yukon, is a man with a zest for living and liquor that would have killed off most men years ago. He is closely related to the principal players of the Klondike gold rush drama and has heard the story of how that first gold nugget was found from the men who were there at the time. Although he is in his seventies, he heads into the bush on a prospecting trip whenever an opportunity turns up.

"This time out, it was some Americans who wanted to go prospecting with a metal detector," said Johns, as he roared with laughter. With the price of gold going up so fast, he explained, all kinds of new gimmicks are being dreamed up to search the northern creeks for the metal that the early miners could not reach with their hand tools.

Johns's cabin, originally the local recording office, was built in 1898. The house has been renovated and extended since 1961, when he moved in.

Johns has lived most of his life in Carcross or in the Indian village of Tagish, twenty-one miles away. There are fewer than two hundred people living in Carcross—a contraction of the old name Caribou Crossing. Thousands more lived there in the gold rush days when the village, which is only fifty miles south of Whitehorse, was on the trail of the Stampeders going from Skagway, Alaska, to the Klondike.

The town is situated at the northern end of Lake Bennett, which extends into B.C. Down this lake, on hand-made boats and rafts, came the would-be miners at the turn of the century. At Carcross, they paddled into the chain of lakes which led them eventually to the Yukon River. At Carcross, on July 29, 1900, the golden spike of the White Pass and Yukon Route railway was driven home, after twenty-seven months of toil. Ever since then, the trains and the tourists they carry have been part of Carcross life.

Visitors stepping off the train here see a village that appears to be frozen in the past. All around are mountains, and the community itself is a cluster of wooden buildings, huddled onto a strip of land between the wind-whipped waters of Lake Bennett and Lake Tagish.

The main street is a dirt road and the sidewalks are wooden. The Matthew Watson general store, painted a cheerful pink and maroon, has old glass-topped showcases. The three-story Caribou Hotel, flags flapping in the breeze, is the heart of the community. In its beer parlor or cocktail lounge, privileged tourists might get to hear Johns recite some of his poems or sing one of his songs. This hotel was the home of Polly, the famous parrot, which allegedly came over the trail of '98 with one of the miners. Polly was muttering obscenities or snoring gently in his cage, surrounded by pots of African violets, right up until the day of his death in the fall of 1972.

The most photographed place in the village is the lakeshore cemetery, where the famous characters of the gold rush all lie buried. The graves have intricately carved, white-painted fences around them and seem like part of a world that died centuries ago. But it only takes a short walk to Johns's cabin beside Lake Bennett to realize that the Klondike drama was not so long ago. And it is still very real to the handsome Indian guide with his white hair, stetson and gorgeously beaded jacket.

"Skookum Jim was my father's cousin, you see, and his sister, Kate, I always called Auntie Kate," said Johns, who was born in 1898 when the stampede to the Klondike began. Skookum Jim was one of the Indian brothers credited with the discovery that started the gold rush. The other brother was Tagish Charley, sometimes known as Dawson Charley. The third man was a white prospector, George Washington Carmack, who was married to the Indians' sister, Kate. She was a Carcross girl, the daughter of a Tagish chief, and the woman known to Johns as Auntie Kate. It is a typical Yukon tale of tangled family relationships.

The most commonly accepted version of the start of

the gold rush begins in 1896, when a white prospector named Robert Henderson found a little gold in a Klondike creek. He passed on the tip to Carmack and the two Indians, who were prospecting together in the same area. At the same time, he made a derogatory remark about Indians that infuriated Carmack, who was proud of his native relatives. Nevertheless, Carmack promised to tell Henderson if he and the Indians had any luck in their hunt for gold in other creeks. Luck they did have, as history has recorded, although it has never been clear whether Carmack or Skookum Jim was the first to find the gold on Rabbit Creek on August 17, 1896. But Carmack did not send word of his find to Henderson, who consequently missed out on the spectacular claims on Rabbit Creek, soon re-named Bonanza Creek.

History may have doubts about who found the first gold on Bonanza Creek, but not Johns. As far as he is concerned, there is not the slightest doubt that it was his relative, Skookum Jim, who started the famous rush.

"I had a lot to do with Skookum Jim in my growing days," said Johns, lighting up his favorite brand of cigar. "I remember him and the others well because, after the gold strikes, they came back here to live. And one of Jim's nephews, Patsy Henderson, told me lots about it. I traveled with Patsy a lot; he was an older man and I learned a lot from him: how to hunt and things like that."

Johns's version of the old story started when Carmack married Kate and prospected around Carcross for a few years. He didn't have much luck so he and his wife set off by boat down the Yukon River to look for gold in more distant creeks.

"George said they'd be back in about a year, but they never showed up," said Johns. "Two years went by and then Jim started worrying about his sister Kate. She and Carmack were a year overdue, so Jim decided to go looking for them." Searching was not easy in those days when the Yukon was a virtually uninhabited wilderness, and Jim had no transportation. So he and Tagish Charley and his seventeen-year-old nephew, Patsy, set to and built a rowing boat. In this small boat, they rowed from Tagish into the Yukon River looking for the missing couple.

"They stopped at different Indian camps along the river, asking questions, and they were told that Kate and Carmack had been through there about one and a half years ago," said Johns. "They'd prospected for a while and then gone on."

The three men in their home-made boat kept on rowing for two weeks, until they reached the Klondike River. Here, the trail was fresh. The Indians at Moosehide, just north of where Dawson City is today, said Carmack was up the Klondike River and would be back in a few days. He was—and Kate was then re-united with her relatives. The Indian men joined Carmack's base camp at the mouth of the Klondike, and everyone began the task of collecting winter feed for themselves and the dogs.

"They were drying salmon and they planned on getting a moose for dried meat," said Johns. "You can always kill a moose any time of the year, but you also put up a lot of dried meat and tallow and stuff like that for the winter. So they went out on a moose hunt up the Klondike and its tributaries."

While Carmack, Jim and Charley hunted, Kate and young Patsy stayed home in base camp. One man usually remained behind in camp on a trip like this to protect the womenfolk and look after the dogs. "You see, a trip like this could take two or three weeks," explained Johns. "The hunters would get some meat, put it in a high cache, and then make a run in another area. When they got some more meat, they'd dry it and put that in a cache, too. In the winter time, when the snow came, they'd go trapping and haul the meat out of the caches."

The hunting party set off in August 1896, and they knew the trip would not be short, because Carmack was forever looking for gold. "The Indians then didn't know what gold was and didn't give a damn either," claimed Johns. "They knew George was always panning the creeks and they saw the gold flakes he got, but it was of no value to them."

The three men had already had their encounter with Robert Henderson and were heading home with packs of meat on their backs, prospecting as they went, when the historic find was made. "A heavy shower hit them and they looked around for good shelter," said Johns. "They got under some trees and waited it out for a while—those showers don't last long. They built a fire and Jim thought he'd brew some tea, so he went down to the nearest creek to get some water.

"As it happened, the creek was flowing over bedrock, kind of cracked up bedrock, a natural riffle you could call it. And he saw those pretty rocks in the water, so he picked up a handful and took them to George. 'Is this what you are looking for, George?' he asked. And George said 'Sure, that's gold.' So that's the way the find was made. That's exactly how it happened."

At any rate, that is how Johns thought it happened. According to Pierre Berton's book *Klondike*, Carmack afterwards insisted that he personally found the gold, although the Indians always maintained it was Skookum Jim. Henderson, the last survivor of the Carmack party, claimed to his dying day that it was the finding of a tiny nugget on top of a side hill by Tagish Charley that led the three men to the creek where Jim subsequently found more gold in the water. The true story of the discovery will never be known.

Despite disagreement about who found the first gold, the three men all shared in the work from that point on. According to Johns, they had no whipsaw with them, so they had to use their axes to make a sluice box. "They just chopped, chopped, chopped until they made some rough boards, three planks about nine or ten feet long, for a sluice box," he recounted. "I don't know if they had nails or not, but they could have pegged and tied the box together instead. So they started sluicing right there and they got some gold, I forget now exactly how much, but it was enough for a grubstake for the winter."

The men thought they were on to something big, so all three staked claims on the creek and then headed back to camp to tell their news to Kate and Patsy. "When I see the gold first, just like I don't care, because I no savvy. I never see gold before," said Patsy when he told the story to tourists in Carcross years later. He also missed out on making a fortune, because he was too young. At that time, a man had to be twenty-one before he could stake a claim and Patsy was still a teenager. Nowadays, the age has been lowered to eighteen.

The day after the men returned to camp, they set off for the mining camp at Forty Mile, close to the Alaska-Yukon border, to record their claims at the recording office there. They were hazy about the location of the border, and at first, according to Johns, they stated that their claims were in Alaska. "It all got straightened out later, I guess," he said. "At any rate, when the men got down to Forty Mile in their boats, the word of the gold naturally got out. People came from all over to Forty Mile, but it took a year for the news to get to the outside world, and it took two years for the stampede to start."

Meanwhile, Carmack and his friends had moved their camp to Bonanza Creek and built a better sluice box. According to Patsy Henderson, they took out gold worth $1,450 in three weeks. Soon it was too cold to work and they had to go back to Forty Mile for the winter. In the spring of 1897, the men were back working their claims again, and the world was not far behind them. In 1898, there were 20,000 men camped around Lake Bennett and Lake Tagish on their way to the goldfields.

Johns was vague about how much his relatives made out of the gold rush, but he remembered that Skookum Jim went on prospecting until his death in 1916. "The last trip he made was to Telegraph Creek in B.C.," he recalled. "On the way back, he got as far as Lower Post and got kinda sick. But he came across country under his own power to Teslin Lake. He was showshoeing, because it was winter and he had just one big dog."

When Jim got to Teslin Lake he was really sick—not surprising considering that he had just walked at least 150 miles on snowshoes, in country where the temperature often dips to fifty below in winter. Adding on the mileage from Telegraph Creek to Lower Post makes the total return trip more like 350 miles.

"Of course, everyone knew Jim at Teslin and everyone helped each other in those days," said Johns. "So they put Jim on a sleigh and brought him with their dog teams to our place at Tagish. We were camped there and trapping, and I was pretty young then. Jim stayed with us for a couple of weeks and then I brought him by dog team to Carcross. Two days later, I put him on the train for Whitehorse and it would have been April by then, I guess." But Skookum Jim's brave struggle to get medical help was in vain. He died of kidney disease in Whitehorse in July 1916.

By then Johns was an experienced young trapper and prospector. "I went to school for four years, but only for six months out of every year," he said. "It was an Anglican mission school and I was good at arithmetic but very poor in writing. I've learned a lot more since I left school because I realized I'd better start teaching myself. So I've always mixed with people who knew a little bit more than me—the professors, doctors and lawyers who went hunting with me. I learned a lot from them. At school they wanted to make a preacher out of me, but my Dad said, 'Oh, no, he's going to be no preacher.' And then he learned me how to hunt."

Johns was one of three boys and two girls, and the only family income was from trapping. "My dad said we had to live off the land, because there were no jobs, nothing at all; you had to make your own work," he said.

"So I had to learn how to hunt, and I loved it. It was good hunting in those days and it's good hunting today. Maybe we've improved the game some—poisoned a few wolves off, you know. But you have to watch that sort of thing. Man sometimes steps in and tries to help nature, but he often does the wrong thing. I did all right trapping because I wasn't lazy. I was always busy and I hate to get beat. So I did good. Some of the other boys would work around town on jobs, but I was always for the bush; I loved the bush and it paid better too.

"When I was a kid, we always got paid for our furs in gold, ten and twenty dollar gold pieces. But before that, it was always a trade deal for goods. Those first fur traders just gave the Indians an IOU for their furs, sometimes a hundred-dollar IOU and sometimes much more. I remember one Indian who always used to come in with five thousand dollars worth of furs at traders' prices, probably worth fifty thousand dollars on the open market, and he only got an IOU. Well, lots of those IOUs got lost or burned up by mistake, so finally the gold came along."

Johns saw plenty of that gold. He was trapping everything from lynx to muskrat and he also sold moose meat to restaurants, because selling game was legal in those days. "I was making way more money than the boys in town. And they were always chasing girls, but I figured that you had to build a nest first, just like the birds, before you looked for a girl," he said.

Johns had another asset going for him as well as energy and that was sharp intelligence. His story of selling his fall muskrats is one example. Johns said he trapped 213 muskrats one fall. Because fall rats brought a lower price than rats trapped in the winter or spring, he did not sell them, but went on trapping through the winter and spring.

"Then, by gosh, for some damn fool reason, I decided to send those fall rats to London, England, and see what I could get for them there," said Johns. "I had the address for the biggest fur traders in the world in London so I

packaged them all up and took them in to the post office."
The man running the post office was also a part-time fur
buyer, and made an offer for the rats himself.

"I forget what he offered me now, but it was about a
hundred and some odd dollars," said Johns. "And I wanted
twenty dollars more than the price he offered me, because
the regular price for fall rats was about thirty cents. I had
the furs all packaged up, addressed, and all I needed was
the stamps." He recalled that the postmaster's name was
Aubrey and that the argument raged for at least a couple of
hours.

" 'Put the stamps on, I want them out of here,' I said
to Aubrey, and he tried and tried and tried to change my
mind. I told him to give me twenty dollars more and he
could have them. But finally, he said 'No,' and so I said,
'Okay, ship them.' "

Johns received a check from London made out in
pounds for the equivalent of $1,050. Shaking with laugh-
ter, Johns recalled: "Right away I went and showed Aubrey
the check."

The check gave Johns the financial means to go into
business for himself, as a guide.

"I found an old copy of *Outdoor Life* magazine at a
campsite. The cover and some of the pages had gone, but I
started looking through it," he said. "I didn't know a thing
about advertising because I didn't have enough education,
but I read through all the classified ads." The advertise-
ments that intrigued Johns were for big game outfitters.
With the money he had acquired from selling his rats in
London, he had enough cash to buy some horses, and, with
his many years of hunting experience, that was basically all
he needed to become a big game guide. "So I put in an
advertisement and said I was a big game outfitter," he said.
"I think it cost two dollars an issue and I put it in for three
months. I wrote out the ad in longhand and I couldn't write
very good. But, by gosh, in three months I got back quite a
few letters."

The worst problem he had was in understanding some of the letters and answering all the questions that people asked. "They asked about the horses and they even asked what weight and draft my boat was. Heck, I didn't know what a draft of a boat meant," said Johns. "I still get crazy letters today. Some people write and ask if they should wear moccasins or snowshoes. Even if they are coming in summer, they'll ask questions like that, no fooling."

Johns was equal to it all. He thinks it was about 1918 when he booked his first hunter—a Pennsylvania man who signed up for a forty-five day hunt at $40 a day. Today the cost would be more like $150 a day. "That first hunter I had was a German-Dutch fellow; there are a lot in that part of the U.S. and they are great hunters. Anyway, he hunted with me for forty-five days and we made good. I just hired one man and I rented my first bunch of horses, about seven of them. We came out with a lot of game and that's what counted," said Johns. He had started on a career that was to last him for the rest of his working life, making him friends in all walks of life and from all parts of the world, as well as earning him a reputation as a first-class guide.

"It was word of mouth that brought me most of my hunters after that," said Johns. "My first hunter came back again and brought a friend with him. Then he came again with his wife and sixteen-year-old son and in a few years, I had all the hunters I could handle."

At first, Johns used horses to transport his supplies, camping equipment and hunters up beyond the timberline of the mountains. In later years, he flew his hunters into a high-level base camp and the hunt was started on horses from there. He had never seen an airplane until 1924, yet he was quick to incorporate planes into his business.

"Before I knew it, I was classed as one of the top ten best guides in the world," said Johns, who could never be accused of false modesty. "My hunters came from all over the world, mostly from the U.S., of course, but also from Europe, Mexico and New Zealand."

Johns's son, Art, joined his father in the business and also became one of the Yukon's top guides. "Johnnie Johns and Son," read their promotional brochure—"Our motto: your success is our success." Johns had quickly learned the art of advertising. In the brochure, he warned prospective customers that two of the few items he did not supply with the hunt were women and booze—"Bring your own," he advised. For game, he offered clients this selection: Dall sheep, giant Yukon moose, Osborn caribou, Rocky Mountain goat, grizzly, black and brown bear, wolverine, wolf, and game birds.

Art is Johns's only son, but he also has two married daughters and seventeen grandchildren at the last count—"more like twenty-five now." His first three wives, now dead or divorced, were Yukon women. Anita, his fourth wife, was originally from Kansas. They met in 1959 in California, when Anita was working in a restaurant and Johns was on a tour with a sports writer.

"They pulled up in front of the restaurant where I worked and there was a press sign on their car," said Anita. "So I sent a couple of my stooges out to find out who was the very impressive looking man in the car. They came back and told me it was Johnnie Johns of the Yukon."

Johnnie and Anita soon got to know each other, and he invited her to come to the Yukon and cook for his camps. When Anita arrived in the Yukon, she ran into a problem with immigration department officials, who said she would be taking a job away from a Canadian. "So Johnnie felt sorry for me and married me," laughed Anita—with her tongue firmly in her cheek.

The north was familiar to her, because she had spent some time in Alaska and she was happy to be back north of the sixtieth parallel. She had ridden and shot before, but had never been big game hunting. "She just fell right into it," said Johns proudly. "She's tops with horses and she's a good shot. She's shot a moose, a bear and a goat."

"He's telling you that, but he never tells me," said

Anita, and her husband interjected—"Well, we don't want you to get too big for your britches." They laughed together and Anita warmly praised Johns' son and daughter-in-law, who had taught her so much about hunting.

Johns has few regrets that his long trips are over, because he is a man who has left very little undone. He can name drop to beat anyone. Prince Philip, Bing Crosby, the late Lyndon Johnson—he has either met or talked to them all. Johns's current dog is named after Prince Philip, who, on a visit to the Yukon, politely asked Johns which hospital he was born in. The startled royal visitor was told in reply: "Under a spruce tree, duke; there weren't no hospitals then."

Another glorious moment that Johns likes to recall was when he took over the floor of New York's Stork Club with one of his notorious compositions—probably "Squaws along the Yukon." He is a born entertainer and, with a receptive audience, can keep up a non-stop patter of songs and jokes for hours.

"Everyone who goes out with me on a trip has a good laugh," he said. "Wherever Johnnie Johns is, there is laughter and happiness." That was another reason for his great success as a big game guide. Many excellent guides can get their hunters most of the animals they want, but there are very few like Johns, who combines superb guiding skill with a personality that spreads a glow over the coldest hunting trip.

Johns was always happiest in the highest reaches of the mountains. On hunting trips, there might have been as many as twenty-one horses in the group: eight saddle horses and the rest carrying packs. Sheep have sharp eyes and Johns preferred his hunters to wear olive drab clothing, so the group was not colorful. Johns always led the way and each horse seemed to know its place in line. The pack train wound its way up steep hillsides, over bogs and across rock slides, but Johns never used a compass; he claimed he would get lost if he did. Many times he stopped the train to go ahead and scout the best route. A base camp was established and then the hunters moved on to set up camps at higher levels. As the horses climbed higher and higher, the mosquitoes and blackflies disappeared and, above timberline, there could even be snow and fog in August.

In the mountains, John's ancestors had hunted sheep with the lance and knife, and he often said he could feel their spirits all around him.

The hunters went on foot for the final stalk of a sheep. The horses were trained to remain exactly where they were until the men returned. Johns kept testing the wind by crumbling some dust, holding it aloft, and dribbling it down into his palm to see which way it was blown. He took his time and carefully scrutinized all the bands of sheep through powerful binoculars. Sometimes he spent as long as an hour watching a sleeping ram and then, when it finally woke and turned its horns, he snorted with disgust, saying, "No, not quite good enough." Johns pointed out to his hunters how sheep teach their young to walk beneath them until they are agile enough to escape from preying eagles. At last, his inspection of the sheep was over and a target was decided on. Then it was up to the hunter to get the game and, under Johns's guidance, he seldom failed.

At night the supper menu was often moose ribs cooked over the fire on green sticks and bannock laced with freshly picked berries. No one could beat Johns's guides when it came to cooking this sort of food, and there was always heaps of it.

The procedure for hunting the shaggy-haired Rocky Mountain goat, which can weigh up to three hundred pounds, often included a trip by canoe or small boat down a lake. The goats live high on rugged cliffs, but it was easy to see as many as a hundred of them in a morning. Shooting one was far from easy and sometimes involved a 2,000-foot climb. By the time the hunt was over it might be dark, and then Johns led the way back to camp. He pitched rocks ahead of him and if they could be heard rolling, the hunters knew it was safe to move on. If there was a long period of silence after a rock was pitched, Johns knew that meant a steep drop, and tried a different route. Sometimes it was as late as 2:30 a.m. when the exhausted hunters fell into their sleeping bags.

Johns shot hundreds of grizzlies during his guiding days, but he never lost his respect for the unpredictable nature of bears. They will either be hard to find or else they will show up uninvited at breakfast time, attracted by the smell of frying bacon. One hunter described Johns as "poetry in motion," as he leaped off his horse and lifted his gun to aim at an approaching bear, all in one swift movement. "Shoot him again," was Johns's advice when his hunters dropped a grizzly, because a wounded bear will often crouch and charge again.

"I can never say that I'm going out on any single day to get a grizzly, but I can do that on a bet with most everything else: sheep, goat, caribou and moose. But not a grizzly," said Johns. Some astounded hunters have sworn they have heard him talk "bear language" to a grizzly he came upon in the middle of a hunt for some other animal, which is often the way bears are encountered. The conversational exchange of huffs, puffs and a few low growls lasted only until Johns ascertained whether the bear was too young to be shot, and the startled animal then took off into the bush looking the picture of offended dignity.

Toward the end of his guiding career, Johns was hunting with trucks, an airplane, horses, pack dogs, back pack, canoes and boats. He would leap his battered pick-up truck over ditches as though it were a horse, and many a Yukon trail has been cleared of boulders by Johns urging on his hunters with the words, "Look at it this way, you won't have to clear it going back."

When Johns sold out, his assets had soared to sixty-five horses, fourteen boats, and enough saddles and harness to equip a cavalry regiment.

In his more than fifty years of guiding, Johns had a

few other jobs on the go as well. For a while, he ran a hotel at Teslin Lake, about seventy-five miles east of Carcross, and was a little vague about why he gave up that enterprise.

His favorite winter job was fur buying for a U.S. company in San Francisco. He went by dog team from Carcross to Telegraph Creek, B.C., a 200-mile journey as the crow flies, but the distance was obviously greater for a man following a winding trail. He was often away from home for two and a half months at a time, and he blamed the long absences for his early marital problems.

"I bought furs all along the way and hit Telegraph Creek at Christmas time to get all the furs that were being brought in there," said Johns. "The traders at Telegraph Creek said they needed fresh money floating around the area and they let me buy all the furs I wanted. So I went in there with twenty thousand dollars cash on my belt—all alone.

"My boss in San Francisco told me never to take cash with me, to pay for everything with checks. But, hell, the Indians in them days didn't know about checks. It was the early thirties. So I had to take cash with me against his orders. But I knew what I was doing. I figured nobody would rob me out in that country and if they did, they'd never get away with it." He was never robbed.

Another part-time occupation that made a few dollars for Johns when he was a young man was guiding for the RCMP. In those days the Mounties usually took an Indian guide with them on long patrols, because the local man's skill in coping with the intense cold as well as his knowledge of the bush were invaluable. And that was how Johns got involved in solving what the RCMP believed was a murder mystery in the 1930s.

The victim was an old man who had been living with his dogs at Little Atlin Lake, about nine miles from Johns's home village of Tagish. When the man's body was found, the head was severed from the torso and looked as though it had been chopped off. The only clothes on the body were top garments, and the man's socks and underwear were scattered all over the place.

A police inspector flew in from Whitehorse to investigate the case and soon decided it was murder. Suspicion fell on a young German man not long in the country, merely because all others living in the area were friends. The only hitch was that there was no motive for the crime, because the old man had no money and little food. Police and doctors tramped all over the site of the alleged murder. Finally, the Carcross police were asked to return for another look and to bring a local Indian with them. The local Indian was Johns.

He set off with the police for Little Atlin Lake, steering his outboard with one hand and turning the pages of a detective magazine with the other. "You see, I had to study up on the case," said Johns, who is never serious about anything for long if he can help it.

When he and the Mounties got to the so-called murder scene, the body had been removed, but the police pointed out where all the evidence had been found. Then Johns got to work. He knew already from a relative that the old man had suffered from a hernia, which sometimes caused him intense pain. And from asking questions, he discovered that a couple of the man's dogs had been loose when the police found the body.

"Well," said Johns, "The man died from exposure and the dogs bit his head off. The dogs were starving to death after the man died, you see, and some got loose and chewed his head off." Naturally the police did not accept his theory right away, so Johns had to prove his reasoning.

"I've fed moose meat to my dogs all my life and they can chop through it just a cleanly as if you'd cut it with a saw," he said. "But when they bite through the neck, there's always one vertebra, a small round piece of bone, that they can't swallow and they can't chew. If my theory is correct, that piece of bone will be around here somewhere." Johns and the police searched the area where the head had been found. "Finally, by gosh, I found it," he said. "Poking around with a stick, there was the little piece I figured should have been left by the dogs."

The police also want to know how Johns accounted for the man's socks and underclothing being scattered around in the weeds, which were all crushed as though a fight had taken place. "Well, that was easy because the weeds were laying in one direction," he replied. "If two men had been fighting, the weeds would have been laying in all kinds of different directions. But there was no hassle. The man was in agony from his rupture and he crawled through the weeds, so they all went in one direction. And he crawled right out of his big woolen socks."

Johns also recalled that at the time the man died, the weather had been very hot during the day. "So I figured he tried to get some shade behind a tree that had blown over—you could see where he had crowded down behind some of the tree roots. And when it got so darn hot in the day, I guess he took off his top clothes and his underwear, because I figure he was out of his mind by that time. Then it got cold at night and he was semi-conscious, so he pulled on the first things he could find, his shirt and pants."

The police needed no more convincing. They closed the case on the basis of Johns's theory. He never played detective again, but there are not many people who can claim they saved a man from being arrested for murder.

Johns had plenty of stories about sickness and death involving other people in the bush, but he has been lucky and has only been really ill once when he was away from home.

"I got cold on my kidney and it was my own fault, really," he admitted. "It was spring and I was out hunting foxes when it happened. On the first night, the ground was all wet and I should have put brush down when I camped. But I was tired and wet and just lay down, and so I got cold on my kidney. Oh gee, I was in misery. I couldn't cough or laugh and I traveled like that for ten days."

Johns's kidney cure was unorthodox, but it worked splendidly for him. This is how he did it. He met up with three friends of his who were also out fox hunting and at night they sat around the fire telling stories. Johns, irrepressible as ever, just had to join in. "They were telling funny stories and I tried hard not to laugh because it hurt so much," he said. "Then someone said something so darn funny that I couldn't help myself, and I laughed. Immediately, I felt as though something had ripped inside of me. That was it—I was okay after that."

On another fox hunting expedition, Johns had to cope with a sick brother-in-law for ten days. There was a chicken pox epidemic raging at the time, but Johns didn't give it much thought before he set off hunting, having already had the disease. However, his brother-in-law was not immune.

The men were way out in the bush miles from home when the brother-in-law felt a headache coming on. But that didn't stop him from diving into an icy lake and swimming out to retrieve a beaver he had shot. It was May, but there was still a lot of ice in the lake. The combination of the freezing dip and the beginnings of chicken pox soon turned him into a very sick man.

"We just had one little fly tent and one pack dog, because our horse had got away on us," said Johns. "We didn't have much provisions either, because we'd left some of our grub at the place where the horse had taken off." So Johns had to be both hunter and nurse. He shot rabbits and ptarmigan with a .22 rifle and made them into a stew to try to get some strength back into the sick man. "But, oh boy, it was really tough because his mouth was all raw on the inside," said Johns. "Finally, we talked and he told me to leave him so that maybe I could get some horses." But Johns would not hear of it, because his brother-in-law was far too sick to look after himself for even a day or two. Then the men decided to give the Turkish bath treatment a try.

"That's how the Indians used to bathe in the olden

days and it's very simple," said Johns. "You take some rocks, roll them into the fire, and get them red hot. Then right close by, you dig a hole and roll the rocks into it when they are hot. You also make a frame of willows over the hole and put a piece of canvas over the top, with an opening just big enough to let the head stick out. Then you put some boughs down over the hole and throw cold water over the rocks, and you get lots of steam.

"So that's what I did for my brother-in-law. I made him comfortable in there—put a little brush down for him and a blanket, and, by golly, it cured him. From then on, he got better. But it was a tough time—it was ten long days staying in one place."

So ended one fox hunting trip, but there were many others, more lucrative ones, because a silver fox fur brought $1,000 in those days. Then came the idea of breeding the animals in captivity, and Johns and his friends caught many a fox for ranchers who planned to set up fox farms. The ranchers' greed finally caught up with them, however. "They overdid it, you see, and raised so many foxes that the price was killed," said Johns. "Now a fox ain't worth more than ten or twenty dollars."

He is very proud of the fact that in all his working life he has only worked for a "boss" for a total of three months. That was when he did section work on the railway because "the natives never got no good jobs," he said. "Outside of those three months, I've been my own boss all my life—like on a hunting trip I'm my own boss, if you see what I mean."

Johns also considered the work he did on the construction of the Alaska Highway in 1942-43 a no-boss job. The 1,523-mile highway winds its way from Dawson Creek, B.C., to Fairbanks, Alaska, and more than five hundred miles of the road are in the Yukon. The gravel highway was originally named the Alcan, because it was jointly constructed by the U.S. and Canada as a military route in case the Japanese invaded during World War II. (The name never stuck and it is known now as the Alaska Highway.) Johns supplied horses and acted as scout in the Yukon for the highway engineers.

"I had about ninety head of horses on that job and we were right out in the bush," said Johns. "Where we blazed trail is where the highway went. Everybody gives me hell because I made the highway crooked, but those were our orders. We had to make it crooked because the government thought the Japanese were getting ready to bomb it. If we'd made it straight, someone else would have come along and put bends in it.

"I've been prospecting a lot since I retired because there's a lot of minerals around here that have been overlooked," Johns said. He pointed to the ore samples over the fireplace and said one contained $800 to $1,000 a ton in silver and the others were four per cent zinc and four per cent lead.

"Now that gold's going so high, there are creeks all over the north that should be gone over again," he said. "When gold was sixteen dollars an ounce, they turned down a lot of these creeks because they weren't a paying proposition. But now they figure gold might climb to a hundred dollars an ounce and there's a lot of people taking interest in gold again. I think we are in for another little gold rush."

Johns's enthusiasm for prospecting is so great that on a recent trip, he and Anita lost track of the time. When they went to the local hotel for a warm-up drink after the cold trip, they discovered it was Sunday, not Saturday.

That anecdote made Johns look at the time. He casually flicked up his sleeves to reveal a watch, made especially for him, that was more like a sculpture than a mere timepiece. On both sides of the face were miniature Dall sheep heads fashioned in gold, and the wristband was set with tiny gold nuggets and jade.

He decided there was time for a drink before dinner and a beer was essential to get his voice in shape for a Johns recital. Everyone in the hotel beer parlor had heard his songs many times, but Johns could never be boring. Within minutes his table was full and he told how he wrote his poem "There Still Is Time" to calm down an impatient hunter who wanted to do everything at once.

"You may be a hundred and five years old some day, but there still is time," said Johns. "Time to fish, time to hunt, time to work, time to play, time to love, time for everything."

The poem began:

> Too swift, too swift, each moment's flight,
> Too soon today is yesterday,
> From sprouting youth of restless fight,
> I fought and came a dusty way.
> Few of my seventy years were gay,
> But life holds many an ample tongue,
> Of sherry, port or rich Tokay.
> It's time to get some drinking done.

The poem flowed on, not quite scanning here and there, and sometimes hard to understand as the words poured out faster and faster.

Finally Johns let rip with his most famous number, "Squaws Along the Yukon," which he said he had "touched up" here and there. He said the song was written originally by a trapper on the Yukon River and was later put to music by a man named Cam Smith. Johns claimed the song was on its way to extinction when he revived it by teaching it to the U.S. soldiers working on the Alaska Highway. Since then, it has been a permanent Yukon favorite.

> There's a salmon-scented girl who sets my head a-whirl
> And she lives up in the Yukon far away.
> Oh, she sleeps out every night beside the camp fire bright
> Then she cuddles up to me and says:
> Oh, youga-youga-youska, which means that I love you,

If you will be my daddy, I will youlaga-youska-you.
Then she placed her hand in mine and I sat her on
   my knee,
Oh, the squaws along the Yukon are good enough
   for me.
Oh, I do love the white girls for they are very nice,
But you can't have the white girls unless you have the
   price.
They are always wanting powder, a lipstick or some
   rouge.
And all my little squaw wants is a pot of mulligan
   stew.
Oh, youga-youga-youska, etc., etc.
She had Indian ways galore, kisses that tasted like
   more,
And a love in the good old-fashioned way.
She surely did look neat with those snowshoes on her
   feet
As she mushed up the old trapline and said:
Oh, youga-youga-youska, etc., etc.

Johns could go on laughing, singing and joking all
night—and many a time has done so. When there's good
company around he will, as he put it, "drink the stars to bed
for fun.
   "I would not trade this north country for any other
land on earth," Johns said. "High up there in the glaciers
where there are no barbed wire fences, it is really living.
And I can say I have lived—that's all that matters."

Chapter 3
Ted Trindell
Trapper

For a trapper living in the bush of northern British Columbia in the early 1930s, the essential ingredient for survival was good health. The nearest doctor could be hundreds of miles away. Ted Trindell knew that very well, so when his appendix began to give him pain, he realized he would have to act fast. In those days swift action meant a bumpy dog-team trip—riding like hell through the bush and hoping and praying there would be medical aid at the end of the trail, before the pain became too great.

Trindell's journey in search of an appendicitis operation has become famous in the north, where almost everyone has a survival-in-the-wilderness story to tell and where medical mercy flights are commonplace. But Trindell's story is unusual, because his was probably the first mercy flight out of the Northwest Territories, and he arranged and paid for it himself.

Trindell, part white and part Slavey Indian, was born in 1902 at Fort Norman beside the Mackenzie River in the Northwest Territories. His five years at church schools gave him more religion than writing and arithmetic and so, like most men of that time in that country, he became a trapper. As he put it, "There was no job, so I went out trapping." At best, the work lasted only four or five months of the year, November to March, and in the summer there was no chance of earning a dollar. So the money earned from those few months of trapping had to last all year.

"The only people who had regular jobs were the Hudson's Bay post clerk and one or two fellows who hauled meat for the company," said Trindell. "But we didn't complain about no work, because that's all we knew. In those days you didn't get no welfare, but there were no game regulations either, so all the game was free."

He trapped for a few years in the Territories, then headed south across the British Columbia border and established a trap line in the Fort Nelson area. "My trap line ran about fifty to sixty miles and I had my main cabin at Deer River, that's about sixty miles north of Fort Nelson," said Trindell. "The only white man in that whole country was the Hudson's Bay man. And there were not many Indians, either. I was always alone in the bush because I didn't have a partner, but I was always too busy with my line to be lonely. My mind was always set on my line. Then, when I got home to the main cabin, I had to cut wood and cook and the day was gone."

Trindell's first wife died and in 1928 he married Bella, an Indian woman who was also born in Fort Norman. Life looked good for the young couple, as long as the fur prices remained steady. He trapped as hard and long as he could every year, then headed home to his wife and cabin.

Ted Trindell
47

In the winter of 1932, the first stabbing pains of appendicitis hit Trindell as he was out on his trap line in the Fort Nelson area. At first, he didn't know what was wrong with him, but he didn't take long to figure it out.

"I packed my gear, left my wife at Nelson Forks, and headed for Fort Simpson up in the Northwest Territories, because I knew there was a doctor there," he said. In Fort Simpson there was also the almost-new St. Margaret's Hospital, built in 1931.

There was another reason why Trindell headed north rather than south in search of medical help. He wanted to be near his relatives in Fort Simpson. "In those days the Indians were superstitious, and if you got sick, they were scared to come around," he said. "If you were dead, you might be lucky if they buried you with a pole or something. So, I figured when I got sick I'd go back to where most of my relatives were and at least I'd get a decent burial."

Nelson Forks to Fort Simpson is a 200-mile cross-country sprint by dog team in winter, and Trindell wasted no time on the trip. He was starting to feel very ill and the pain was constant. St. Margaret's Hospital looked like the end of the rainbow when he drove his tired dogs into town. He headed straight for the hospital and was quickly admitted, but that was as far as he got.

"The doctor said he couldn't tackle an operation, because he didn't have a certified nurse to help him," said Trindell. "At least, that was the story he told me. He just didn't know what to do about me, so I lay there in bed and got weaker and weaker." He stayed in the hospital for a month, wondering if he would ever leave there alive. "Finally, one day I was feeling pretty tough and I said to the doctor, 'What are you going to do with me—operate or not? If not, I'll have to go back and die at home.' But I didn't get an answer—the doctor didn't know what to do."

Trindell then realized his only hope of surviving was to get to a properly staffed hospital in Edmonton. That meant a journey of about seven hundred miles, which was certain death for a man in his condition if he attempted it by dog team. There was a plane connection between Fort Simpson and Edmonton, but only once a month, and by this time even a week's delay could have been fatal. The only thing to do was to charter a plane.

Today a charter would be comparatively easy even in the high Arctic, but in 1932 in the Northwest Territories it was extremely unusual. After all, it had been only eleven years previously that the first aircraft had even flown so far north.

Pioneer flights relied heavily on the traditional wing and a prayer to get in and out of the sky, but they were successful enough to make flying in the far north a reality. The first commercial company, Mackenzie Air Service Ltd., had just been formed, so Trindell turned to it for help. The fledgling company agreed to take him to Edmonton for the astronomical sum of $1,000. For the company to charter a plane to a white business executive in those days was unusual. To charter to a sick Metis trapper was unheard of.

"I had to sell all my equipment, all my trapping outfit, to get that thousand dollars and make a deal with the pilot. It cleaned me right out," said Trindell. The tiny Mackenzie Air plane took off from Fort Simpson with the charter customer, stony broke and in the last stages of appendicitis, strapped into the passenger seat. Within hours, Trindell was in hospital in Edmonton and an operation was underway—in the proverbial nick of time.

"I got the appendix yanked out and in eight days I was okay," he recalled. As he felt his strength returning, there was no way anyone could have kept him in hospital for a long convalescence. The only thing he wanted to do was to get back to his wife as soon as possible.

"You couldn't phone out in those days—we just had morse code messages for communications," he said. So Bella, whom Trindell had left in the care of the Hudson's Bay post at Nelson Forks two months previously, had no way of knowing whether her husband was alive or dead. "When I left her at Nelson Forks, I didn't know if we'd ever meet again," said Trindell. "She'd had a miscarriage just before I left, so I had to get back to her as quick as possible."

The journey from Edmonton back to Bella took him the best part of a month, because he had no money left to pay for any kind of transportation. He hitched rides with dog teams from Edmonton to Spirit River, Alberta, and then on to Fort St. John, B.C., until he came to a point seventy-five miles south of Fort Nelson. "From there, another fellow and I walked into Fort Nelson and then gradually I got home to Nelson Forks," said Trindell. "The operation was bothering me a bit, but I made out all right. By the time I got back, I'd been away three months."

He and Bella were finally reunited, and the fact that they were both alive was reason enough to be joyful. They certainly did not have anything else to celebrate. Not only did they not have a cent but, far worse for a trapper, they had no equipment. Trindell had sold it all to pay for his charter flight.

"But as soon as spring came, I went out beaver hunting at Nelson Forks," he said. "It was a good spring and a pretty good convalescence—I got fifty beaver. Beaver skins were bringing around thirty, forty, and fifty dollars then, which was fair money, and there were lots of beaver around in those days." So Trindell was able to pay all his bills and in 1933, he and Bella headed back to Fort Simpson, the place where they felt most at home.

In the early 1930s, Trindell had found Fort Nelson a "very primitive place" and he was happy to be back in the old fur trading center of Fort Simpson, where the Mackenzie joins the Liard River. Fort Simpson, although more than a hundred miles north of the B.C.-N.W.T. border, was founded in 1804 and is the oldest continuously occupied site on the Mackenzie River. Trindell considered it a far more civilized place than Fort Nelson, which was not much more than a "little bit of a moccasin road" on the banks of the Fort Nelson River, and where the only white man for miles around was the Hudson's Bay factor. "I remember snaring rabbits where the airport at Fort Nelson is today," said Trindell. "But, my God, they're more civilized in Fort Nelson than we are now."

The Trindells, although they were both born in Fort Norman, first met in Fort Simpson. And Trindell likes to tell the story of how he married Bella, after he had been stood up by another girl in Edmonton. Even in his seventies, he could not resist giving his wife a little gentle teasing about that long-ago romance.

"I met this girl in Edmonton and told her I'd be back in two years to marry her," he said. "But, when I went back, she'd gone and married someone else. Then, I figured all women are the same anyway, so I married Bella instead." And he gave his wife a private smile as he said it because they both knew he did not mean it. And she smiled back, because she had heard the story many times before.

When the couple arrived back in Fort Simpson in 1933, they were still trying to recover from the financial disaster of Trindell's operation. "I had to start all over again from nothing and I went to all the stores for help, but the best I could do was a hundred-dollar grubstake [money to finance a trapping or prospecting trip]," he said. "That's all I could get, so with that and thirty-three traps I went about sixty miles up the Liard River and started trapping. I used a lot of snares as well as the traps and I built a little cabin and a meat cache. By Christmas I came in with twelve hundred dollars, and so I was able to buy back all my equipment.

Trindell and Bella have no children of their own. They lost two baby boys—one died at birth and the other at six months old. Both babies were born at the same Fort Simpson hospital which had failed to help Trindell in 1932. "In those days, you were lucky if you lived and, if not, you died," he said. "Live or die—there was no choice because there were no doctors."

Trindell was a little bitter about the ease with which

medical care is available today. It all came too late to help his family. "Today, if you break your little finger the government flies you to Edmonton and nothing's said—it's all free," he said. "And when I think of all that I had to go through. People today don't even think the same way we did, and it's not really surprising because today things are so easy."

Trindell, like most men in the Fort Simpson area, has tried his luck at looking for the fabled gold of the Nahanni River. Many have searched for the gold, but no one has found more than a few ounces of it and lived to tell the tale. "Me and a white guy went up into the mountains to look for the Nahanni gold in 1934," said Trindell. "Tex Hughes was the fellow's name and he only took a .22 with him, though I warned him to take a good rifle because we might run into trouble. He just laughed at me and said Indians were always scared of bears." Hughes was destined to learn the hard way.

The two men were deep in Nahanni country one evening, when they were chased by a grizzly. Hughes fired, but the single shot in his rifle only wounded the bear in the leg, enraging the animal even more. Trindell's eight dogs immediately surrounded the bear, which was fine—except that all the men's ammunitition was in a pack on one of the dogs. So Trindell had to sneak up to within a few feet of the snarling, pawing grizzly and grab the ammunition from the dog's back. Hughes was then all set to let rip with a hail of bullets at the wounded bear, but Trindell held him back.

"No," I told him. "Those are good dogs. Don't you dare try to shoot while the bear is in the middle of them."

But it was all Trindell could do to restrain Hughes from pulling the trigger until the dogs had maneuvered the bear into a small stream. Then there was a clear line of fire. The men shot the grizzly through the head and none of the dogs was injured.

"Hughes was delighted and he said we were going to have bear steak for supper," said Trindell. "But I said nothing doing, I couldn't have eaten any of that bear even if I'd been starving. I couldn't eat anything that had scared me as much as that bear did. So I just cut two claws off the bear and gave one to Hughes and kept one for myself."

The Trindell-Hughes gold expedition was not successful. They found no gold and they got along together so badly that at one point they contemplated splitting up and returning independently to Fort Simpson. But Trindell swiftly dismissed that idea. The notorious Nahanni River and its Deadmen's Valley had been the grave of too many men who died mysterious deaths, and Trindell did not want to add to the legends.

"If one of us had got home and the other had gone missing, well, the guy who got home would have had a lot of explanations to make," he said. "So I said we must stick together." And stick together they did, as they climbed into the mountains and floated back down the Cariboo River on a hand-made raft. But their relations were so strained that Trindell took to carrying a loaded gun with the safety catch off all the time. "It was nip and tuck with Hughes," he said. "And I said to myself, my life is just as sweet as his. But luckily we got back all right. It was the toughest trip I've ever went on and I'll never go into the mountains again with a white man. I've been offered five and ten dollars a day to go on prospecting trips with white men many times since then, but I always say no—not even if they paid me a hundred dollars a day would I go through that experience again."

Trindell is convinced the only gold in the Nahanni area is placer gold—"and God knows where that is." Personally, he has had enough of mineral prospecting, which is a long grind of "stake and re-stake, stake and re-stake" with no guarantee of return for all of the work. "I did bite many times at prospecting a few years ago, but I was spending so much money on it that my wife got mad and so I quit," he said. "It's always chasing rainbows, you know. It's a bad sickness, when it gets hold of you. It gets into your

Ted Trindell
53

blood and the big fortune is always around the corner."

Now that he is retired, what Trindell really misses are his dogs, which he sold when he gave up trapping around 1960. "I had some beautiful dogs and I always believed in feeding them properly and keeping them pepped up," he said. And with his tongue in his cheek he added: "Like I tell my wife, when I had a team of dogs my family was starving; now I've got rid of the dogs and the family's eating again. That's about the size of it."

In his book, *Men of the True North*, Dick Turner of Fort Simpson recalled many stories of Trindell and his dogs. He claimed he once saw the dogs drag Trindell along for a mile before they would slow down enough to let him scramble onto the sleigh.

Wrote Turner:

> I think the best dog team I ever saw belonged to Ted when he was trapping near us on the Long Reach. The leader was a Husky called Princess Charlotte and the wheeler was Nigger, a large black German shepherd which was exceedingly bouncy and always ready to go. In the morning Nigger would strain at his tie chain and open and close his mouth in loud whines in an absolute frenzy to get going.
>
> Meanwhile, Charlotte sat on her haunches with a bored expression on her face and would step daintily to her place in the lead when called. When Ted snapped the rope she was off like a shot, with Ted hanging on for grim death. Needless to say, it was part of his religion to feed his dogs well.

While trapping in the bush, Trindell has brushed close to death a dozen times: he has been taken sick, gone hungry, been surrounded by wolves, chased by a bear, and stranded with a broken snowmobile. Next to his epic battle with appendicitis, Trindell's worst illness was a mysterious ailment which flattened him for a month.

"It started when I'd shot a moose and was about ten or fifteen miles from camp on my way home," he said. "I started sweating and soon I was soaking wet. It was winter and the temperature was about thirty below, so I made a huge fire, took all my clothes off, wrapped myself in an eiderdown, and dried my clothes in front of the fire. Then I had to get back home. I put my clothes on again and to keep from getting too cold I ran beside the sleigh for a little bit, then I rode, then I ran, then I rode, and I kept this up until I got home.

"When I reached the cabin I started sweating again, and never stopped for thirty days. Our cabin was snowed in, there wasn't a soul around, and no doctor, of course. I figured I had pneumonia because I had no pain, but I kept sweating, water was just dripping off my legs. Finally, I got mad. I got a tub full of water, threw a pound of mustard in it, climbed in, and started sweating again. When I got out of the tub I fell onto the bed, and my ears were ringing. I went to sleep then, and when I woke up the sweating had gone. The mustard killed it and I was cured. To this day, I don't really know what it was that I had."

Trindell went hungry in the bush only once, and once was enough. "I've smartened up since then," he said. "It's terrible to be hungry; you get weak and your mind wanders, and you really suffer. When it happened to me, I made a promise to myself that it would never happen again. Some people depend on getting their food from the bush, but not me. Now, I always make sure I have my food in a bag—not running in the bush."

In 1972, the only place in Canada where there was a bounty on wolves was the Northwest Territories and Trindell reckoned the government got full value for every forty dollars it paid out. He did not have a grain of sympathy for wolf lovers. "As far as I'm concerned, all the wolves in the world could disappear and we'd be better off," he said. "They are nothing but a nuisance. Many people believe wolves won't tackle human beings, but that's not true. I'd like to see them wiped off the map and the same goes for wolverines and bears. The world would get along very well without them. Wolverines will steal anything, whether they need it or not. They steal fur and destroy it or just carry it away, and I don't know how much fur they've stolen from me.

"And bears are just as bad. They smash cabins and steal and destroy. These three animals are the bad ones of the bush. As for wolves, I've never been tackled by one myself, but I know men who have been. I know two guys who were treed by wolves. These guys were just setting beaver traps and the damn wolves made for them, so they had to climb trees. Myself, I've been amongst a lot of wolves and I used to carry four hundred and five hundred rounds of ammunition all the time, because I just didn't feel safe. The wolves used to go around in packs, maybe twenty-five, thirty, or forty in a pack, and they hung around the trees when I was on my trap line. I figured I was quite brave, but in the end I quit that country because the wolves got so thick. I couldn't take it any more."

With fur prices as high as they have been in recent years—fifty to sixty dollars for lynx, and seventy dollars including the bounty for a wolf—Trindell reckoned he would now be on easy street if he had continued trapping with a snowmobile instead of quitting in 1962 when prices were very low. On the other hand, he might have died of exposure on the trail. Snowmobiles, in Trindell's experience, have such a high rate of mechanical failure that he has resisted the temptations of big money in furs for the more realistic attraction of staying alive.

"A few years ago, my snowmobile broke down when I was about eighty miles out in the bush," he said. "It was winter and the temperature was about thirty or forty below and I just couldn't get it going again. So I had to walk back home and spent three nights on the trail. Luckily I had enough food with me or I might have been in trouble."

Even then, Trindell was better off than the woman

he once knew who had her baby in the wilderness—all by herself in a tent. "My wife and I were out hunting with this girl and her husband, and she thought she might be near to having the baby," said Trindell. "We just made it back to camp with her and pitched a tent and then we went four miles to the nearest village to get help. My wife offered to stay with her, but she wouldn't have it. So she had the baby all alone, while we were off walking to the village. This sort of thing used to go on all the time. The girls were taught by their mothers how to look after themselves. It's not like that today."

Trindell is, above all else, an expremely practical man. He welcomes new advances in technology like the snowmobile, but only makes use of them when he is sure they can be trusted. He likes many of the advantages of civilization, but is sick at heart about the havoc that liquor is causing among the Indians of the north. He is a man with a great respect for the law, and when he sees a wrong he attempts to find a democratic way to set it right. His involvement in Fort Simpson's new Metis Association, which hopes to aid the local Metis people, is typical of Trindell's approach to a problem.

Years ago when the trappers of the Northwest Territories were frustrated by what they felt were pointless government regulations and sometimes insufficient regulations, Trindell was one of the founder members of a trappers' association. The trappers had several meetings with the game warden and, eventually, the regulations were changed so that everyone ended up happy.

Although Trindell is in his seventies, he has little time for his contemporaries who spend their lives sitting around talking about the old days. He works for the federal goverment, spreading information throughout the community on the proposed Mackenzie Valley pipeline.

"It's sort of research I'm doing, finding out how the pipeline will affect the natives. I ask them if they are prepared to get some more education, so that they'll be able to

Ted Trindell
57

fit into the new jobs when they come," he said. "We're trying to find out exactly what impact the pipeline will have on the people here. We're trying to prepare them for what might happen, so that they can cope with it. It sure is a full-time job.

"If the pipeline does come, it will pass very close to here, but I don't think it will have much effect on the environment. People say they are worried about the fish, but there aren't too many fish in the river here. Farther up the river around Wrigley it might be different, because they do get a lot of fish there. But I really don't think the pipeline will hurt too much and I'm sure it's going to come."

Although Trindell was convinced that development will come to the north, like it or not, he was far from sure that the Indians will learn to live with it. "I think things are happening too fast for us, and we were much happier in the old days," he said. "The present situation is called development and civilization, but to most of us it is really exploitation. The trouble is the natives don't have the knowledge and ability to cope with the new life. We used to live on the land and had to be experts in outwitting animals in order to make a living. Everyone knew how to handle the situation then. Men were experts in hunting, women knew their work, and kids learned how to do things that suited their way of life. But now everything is upset for the natives."

Chapter 4
Jack Ardill
Farmer

When the Scottish fur trader Alexander Mackenzie began his journey by birchbark canoe up the Peace River in 1792, he was heading into country no white man had seen before. Mackenzie struggled through rapids which turned the river into a sheet of frothing white water as far as the eye could see. He helped his men portage around a canyon, dragging their canoe through a thick spruce forest. And he enjoyed the river when its wide, smooth waters flowed between huge banks of sand and gravel in a valley of trees and wild roses.

The Peace looked exactly the same 127 years later in 1919 to a young homesteader. That was the year when Jack Ardill joined other homesteaders along the banks of the

Peace, where it makes its comparatively brief 100-mile plunge across northeastern B.C. before entering Alberta. The potential farm land of British Columbia's Peace River country was what attracted settlers there in the first place. Wheat that was only three inches high in the beginning of June would be five feet tall and turning by the end of July, because the soil was rich and during those two months, the days so far north were very long. Although the crops proved splendid, transportation was both difficult and expensive, because the railroad was between a hundred and two hundred miles away. As a result many homesteaders left the land which had taken them so long to reach.

But not Ardill. He had survived the First World War and had roughed it on a Cariboo ranch as early as 1909. He was too tough to quit, despite the problems facing Peace River settlers at the start of this century. Ardill was gentle and softspoken, a modest man who never flaunted his achievements, and it was hard to envisage him as a frontiersman who had hacked a home, a farm, and a ranch out of the wilderness. He preferred to talk about his family, the beauty of his beloved Peace River, and the changes that have come to a land that was once completely isolated.

The turn-off to the Ardill ranch at Farrell Creek near Fort St. John is easy to miss because the sign is so small. The ranch covers about 4,000 acres of deeded land and 30,000 acres of leased land. Some of the acreage is in crops and the rest supports about fifty horses and five hundred head of cattle, mostly top quality Herefords.

Jack Ardill died in 1975, but until then he lived with his wife, Betty, and their bachelor son, John, in a rambling wooden house at the edge of a cliff, with the Peace River winding through a broad valley 250 to 300 feet below. The river dominates the landscape. Around the house are red-painted ranch buildings and a garden of flower beds and lilac bushes. Through a stand of trees can be seen the home of Dick Ardill, another of the couple's three sons. The Ardill ranch is, of course, a family affair.

Jack Ardill was born in Sligo on the west coast of Ireland and his father was a canon of the Church of Ireland. Young Jack was headed for university and probably a clerical career in a world of culture and gentle living. But Latin put an end to those plans.

"I could manage the Greek, but Latin and I disagree, so I told my father I was going to Canada," said Ardill. He made it sound normal for an Irish teenager to suddenly up and leave the shelter of his family in 1909 and head for the new world. But there were probably many words between the generations before the youngster finally embarked for Canada with his passage paid and $25 in his pocket from his father.

"I have never regretted it," said Ardill, who was a slight, frail-looking man in his eighties, with a gracious courtesy that is typical of his generation. A family friend of the Ardills had come out to British Columbia in the late 1800s and started a ranch in the Cariboo at Cache Creek, so that was where the young man headed. He spent three years there learning about farming and ranching in Canada. He had a lot to learn, because the life of an Irish schoolboy with his nose in a Latin book was totally removed from that of a western cowboy. The only thing he found easy was riding, because he had spent many hours on the backs of Irish donkeys.

"I stayed on the ranch until 1912 and then I got footloose and wanted to see what the country was like," said Ardill. "Nobody was expecting a war in those days, so I went wandering and met up with another fellow, and together we took in the Calgary Stampede. It was fun but it was dangerous, too, because it was a pretty wild and woolly affair. But it was a wonderful thing to see because in those days there was plenty of room to walk around and see things. Nowadays it's a crazy place."

After the 1912 Stampede the young men headed east and did some grain threshing in Saskatchewan and

Alberta. As winter approached they decided to take a look at the north, so they went to Athabasca, about eighty miles north of Edmonton, and had a go at homesteading. "But the place wasn't what I wanted at all," said Ardill who, even at this stage, had very definite ideas about the sort of land he was looking for, land on which to settle and put down roots. So he moved north again when he found a job on the construction of a telegraph line to Fort McMurray, Alberta.

"It only paid two dollars a day plus board, but that was good money in those days," he said. "It was winter and we lived in tents all the time, though the temperature often went to forty below. But when you are young, forty or fifty below doesn't make any difference. We had to dig four holes a day two feet deep and the ground was frozen hard."

When the line to Fort McMurray was completed, Ardill went back to Athabasca and from there got a job surveying what was then known as Township 106 and later as the Great Tar Sands. While he was working on this job, he met some men who had surveyed the boundaries of the Peace River Block, that section of the Peace River country lying in B.C. The 10,000-square-mile area includes the communities of Fort St. John, Hudson Hope, Dawson Creek, and Pouce Coupe. From these Peace River surveyors, Ardill heard stories of a rich and fertile land that was there for the taking. He decided to see it for himself as soon as possible, not knowing at the time that he would have to fight a war first. War was declared in August 1914.

"I stayed around Fort McMurray trapping for the winter of 1914-1915 with my partner who was an American," he said. "Then in the spring, we went out and my partner headed for the U.S. and I went to Edmonton and joined up." Ardill was soon shipped overseas. He ended up shot through the knee and with thirty-seven bits of shrapnel in his left side.

But how it happened was not a story easily pried out of Ardill. As far as he was concerned, the war was not a subject for discussion, and his memories of it were strictly private. The only happy thing that happened to him during 1914-1918 was his meeting with his future wife. He was stationed in Holland when he met Betty at her father's seaside resort home at Scheveningen near the Hague. At first Ardill hesitated about marriage because he had no money and no home in Canada to which to take her. "You don't save any money in the army, not by a darn sight," he said. "But we talked things over and decided to get married anyway. We spent five or six months in Holland and then headed back to Canada."

In Ardill's mind during the long trip home were the stories of the Peace told him by his old survey partners. He was determined to homestead, and the Peace River country with its plentiful game and water was going to be the place.

"We left Edmonton on August twenty-fifth, 1919, for Peace River Town and stayed over there for a few days," said Ardill. "Then we headed up the Peace on the stern-wheeler *Pine Pass of Winnipeg* for Fort St. John." The *Pine Pass* was a famous old boat, but she had seen better days, and the 240-mile journey from Peace River Town, Alberta, to Fort St. John, B.C., was no luxury cruise. Ardill slept on deck while his bride shared a cabin with another woman. The trip was scarcely a honeymoon, but it was a pleasant introduction to the land that would soon be the Ardills' home. The early fall colors of the trees were brilliant, and the newlyweds stood on deck gazing intently at the passing scenery in the hope of spotting a suitable homestead site. On September 1, they arrived at Fort St. John, an old Hudson's Bay Company fort that had been founded in 1805, and found themselves in a rugged little community tucked between the river and the bush.

The young couple rented a cabin, sorted themselves out, and then set off to explore the countryside. They rented horses and began their search for land. "We spent about ten days in the beautiful virgin country, and the whole place was wide open," recalled Ardill. "There were only half a dozen settlers down along the banks of the Peace." In fact, by 1921 the population of the entire Peace River Block was only 1,600.

"My wife liked it—she liked the adventure," said Ardill. "But she thought we had some nerve, and I guess we did." Actually, Mrs. Ardill had enough "nerve" for ten women. She was a city girl who had never been on a horse before, and she was already several months pregnant. But through some very tough times she never lost her courage.

The Ardills found plenty of land suitable for farming, but little of it had been surveyed. Eventually, they turned their horses back to Fort St. John and decided to try exploring the river for a change. They rented a canoe, piled it up with their belongings, and started paddling upstream. They liked the look of an area that is now called Bear Flat, but were discouraged to find that all the suitable land had already been snatched up. "It was just being held by trappers who didn't want settlers coming," said Ardill with a tinge of the bitterness he must have felt in 1919.

Once again the young people turned around and headed back for Fort St. John. By now summer had turned into fall and the Ardills still did not know where they were going to spend the winter. At Fort St. John they boarded their old friend the sternwheeler *Pine Pass of Winnipeg* and booked passage for Hudson Hope, the head of navigation on the Peace, about sixty miles upstream.

Hudson Hope was a Hudson's Bay trading post, and not much else, well situated in the foothills of the Rockies. Many old trappers lived there with Indian wives. One of these trappers, a Scotsman named Harry Garbett, befriended the Ardills, lent them a cabin, and took them on a pack train trip south of the Peace to Moberley Lake. "It was beautiful country with hills for winter pasture, but we ran up against the same old drawback—it wasn't surveyed," said Ardill. "Then on October fourteenth, winter arrived, cold and snowy, so we headed back to Hudson Hope and settled down for the winter."

While Mrs. Ardill attempted to turn a drafty old log cabin into a cosy home, her husband struck up a friendship with an old-timer named Dudley Shaw, who had a long trapline in the surrounding countryside. The friendship soon resulted in an offer to share the trap line, so at last Ardill had a source of income. It was a good winter for game and Ardill made the best of it. But when February came, the young couple knew they would have to head for civilization immediately if Mrs. Ardill was going to have medical aid for the birth of her first child.

"It was forty below when we left Hudson Hope on February second, 1920," said Ardill. "We left with the mailman on a sleigh down the Peace to Fort St. John and there was about three feet of snow on top of the river ice." Mrs. Ardill, twenty-four years old and eight-and-a-half months pregnant, was bundled up with all the clothes she owned: on her feet were the Wellington boots she had had the foresight to buy before arriving in British Columbia.

The strange procession of people and dogs raced over the frozen river that frigid February. They spent the first night at Bear Flat and the second night at Fort St. John. But on the morning of the third day the barometer had dropped so low that the mailman refused to continue. A delay was out of the question for the Ardills, however, so they hired a man and a sleigh to take them on to the next settlement. A doctor was available there, but was "indisposed," as Ardill discreetly put it more than fifty years later. A drunk doctor is worse than no doctor at all, so the Ardills pushed on to Spirit River, Alberta, where the railway tracks were a welcome sight.

The following day, the Ardills climbed on board a train and their first child, John, was born in an Edmonton hospital on February 22, 1920. "We just made it in time and, oh boy, we were scared we might be too late," said Ardill.

The Peace River country in mid-winter was no place for a new mother and baby, so Ardill left his little family behind in Edmonton while he returned to find a homestead. In Spirit River, he bought a horse and saddle, and rode back to the cabin and trap line at Hudson Hope. Every spare moment he spent looking for land, talking to old-timers, and striding along the banks of the Peace. Finally, his determination was rewarded. He found exactly what he wanted twenty miles east of Hudson Hope at Farrell Creek—a lush spread of fertile land atop the river bank.

"The river has proved to be a great asset over the years," said Ardill. "For a long time, it was the main means of transportation in summer and winter because there were no roads—just a pack trail." It is not until late spring that the ice in the Peace goes out and it was May 6, 1920, before Ardill could take to the river to go and file his homestead claim. He floated downstream with a couple of trappers on a home-made raft and paddled himself ashore between great slabs of ice at Peace River Town. There he filed an application for a quarter-section and a soldier's land grant, which together gave him 220 acres. The Soldiers Settlement Board of Canada gave financial help to ex-soldiers to buy machinery and animals, and the debt did not have to be paid back for twenty-five years. And so the Ardill ranch was under way.

The family was reunited in Edmonton and then began a shopping expedition lasting almost two months. "I bought a team of horses, a light saddle horse, a cow and calf, chickens, a plough, a mowing machine, a rake, some furniture, a tent, and a grub stake for a year," said Ardill. The family was allowed to pack this mountain of equipment into a boxcar and transport it from Edmonton to Peace River Town for $100 under a special agreement with the railway for the freighting of "settlers' effects." It seemed like the transportation bargain of the century, until the train ran out of track eight miles outside Peace River Town.

"There was a wash-out, so the only thing we could do was unload the boxcar and haul our freight into town," said Ardill. "I got the loan of a wagon and hitched up my team and got the first load into town in dandy style. But the next day, when I was taking the second load into town, I bumped into a bad spot on the road and the rack on the front of the wagon broke. The whole load came down and me with it. There was furniture and machinery all over the place, and the horses took off with the empty wagon."

Dusty, dirty, bruised, and angry, Ardill limped into town and caught up with the wagon and team. Back he trudged, reloaded, and hauled everything down to the dock where he and his family would board the sternwheeler to take them to their homestead. Next day, only the cow and calf and a few last oddments remained to be brought down to the dock and Ardill thought he had plenty of time. He was wrong. As he led the animals around the last bend in the road, he saw the sternwheeler *D.A. Thomas* pulling away from the dock. The Ardills had missed the boat. There was only one thing to be done—wait for the next boat in two weeks' time.

"The problem was we didn't have any money, so I had to sell the saddle horse for a hundred and fifty dollars to keep us going in those two weeks, and we spent the time living in a tent," said Ardill. The next time the *D.A. Thomas* pulled out of Peace River Town, the family and all their worldly possessions were safely on board.

"Those were good old days on the *D.A. Thomas*, and my wife and the new baby didn't mind the trip at all," said Ardill. "We'd start out about eight o'clock in the morning and pull into shore at a logging camp in the evening. We needed logs for fuel and there were men all along the river cutting wood. We'd build a big camp fire at night and sit around telling stories. We had lots of time and there was no rush. We got stuck a few times on gravel bars in the river, but that was all in a day's work."

After four days on the river, the sternwheeler reached Farrell Creek, the site of the Ardill homestead. The pioneering days had begun. "They dumped all our stuff from the boat right out on the river bank and we had to get it to the top of the cliff, which was straight up about two hundred and fifty or three hundred feet," said Ardill. "So I hitched up the horses and took up the cow and calf, our camping equipment and, last but not least, John, who wasn't six months old yet." Up went the tent, the cow and calf were tethered to a tree because there was no place to turn them loose, and the exhausted family went to bed.

"But we'd only been in bed about an hour when there was the bang, bang, bang of thunder and a big storm blew up," said Ardill. "The rain was terribly heavy and the wind was so strong it blew the tent down."

Husband and wife battled in the deluge to put the tent up again and they were drenched to the skin by the time they huddled down under the canvas shelter for the second time that night. The hours until dawn were long and miserable. The following day they found an old trapper's shack nearby which was half collapsed but at least had a solid roof. So they patched it up temporarily and moved in until they had time to build their own cabin. The next problem was getting the equipment and supplies from the river bank to the cliff top. To do this, Ardill made a stone boat—a flat wooden sledge without wheels which was pulled by horses.

"And we also had a stroke of luck because a couple of Indians came along the trail and they talked what you might call pidgin English," he said. "I asked them if they would work with us, and they helped us get the farm machinery and the heavy cookstove to the top. Then I asked them if they would cut logs for me for two dollars a day for the two of them. They said okay and we were fortunate because they turned out to be good workers. So they cut poplar logs for me with my saw and axe, and then my wife and I put up the house."

The Ardills built a 12 by 16 foot cabin roofed with tarpaper and dirt and fitted with a floor made out of wooden packing cases. "I'd brought a door and windows with me in the freight, so pretty soon our house was all set for the coming winter," he said. "I was used to using an axe because of all the surveying jobs I'd had, but it was another new experience for my wife. My poor wife learned lots of new things in those days. I shot some chickens and slung them over to her to clean. She'd never cleaned a chicken before in her life. And it was me who taught her how to make bread for the first time."

When the cabin was finished, the Ardills had time to catch their breath and take a good look around their homestead. What they saw was rich, fertile land, but it also represented years of future toil for them both. "It was lovely land, you see, but it was all bush," said Ardill. "There were some open spots, but most of the land was fairly heavily bushed, and it all had to be ploughed under with teams of horses or cut down."

An enclosure for the animals was next on Ardill's agenda and he achieved this by digging into a hill of gumbo clay and making a sort of dugout shelter for them. With the approach of winter, hay for animal feed was another top priority, and the meadows of peavine and wild grass were the answer. "So we started in mowing, and all went well until I hit a hidden stump and broke the knife," said Ardill. "It was goodbye mower for that year, because there wasn't a chance of getting it repaired. So the old scythe came in handy then, but it sure was a backbreaker."

Although Ardill had filed a homestead claim, he had to make certain "improvements," as the government termed them, before he was given final title to his land. Within the first three years a habitable house had to be erected, thirty acres had to be cultivated, and buildings put up for stock, of which there had to be five head in the first year and ten in the second year.

"We had more good luck in that first winter, when I met up with an old-timer named Henry Farrell who come here in 1910—the creek on our property is named after him," said Ardill. "I did some work for him with my team and he asked me if I could trap. Of course I'd trapped for several years, so that was no problem, and he offered me half his trap line. He was seventy years old then and he didn't want the whole line himself."

Ardill was delighted, because good prices were being paid for fur at that time, and the money would be more than welcome. When winter was over, he moved the family cabin about a quarter of a mile so that it was close to a spring of fresh water. The move seemed sensible at the time, but Ardill did not know that he had located the cabin in the middle of an ancient Indian camping ground. The first he knew of it was when a group of Indians rode up and made camp under a huge old jackpine tree, which was only twenty feet from the Ardill cabin door. "There were about ten buck Indians with their squaws, papooses and dogs," he said. "The leading buck pulled up and told me to tie up my chickens, or else his dogs would eat them."

This ultimatum put Ardill in a very difficult position. He could not run around tying up all his chickens every time a group of Indians came down the trail. On the other hand, he could not afford to lose the chickens. So he and the Indians began a war of nerves.

"I took down my rifle and walked over to the chicken coop and sat down with the gun over my knee," said Ardill. "The Indians looked at me, but I said nothing, so they moved off to the big jackpine tree and started unpacking. But they never took the ties off the dogs' noses." He was referring to the strings which Indians at that time often used to tie around their dogs' noses when the animals were traveling. When he saw that the dogs were going to remain muzzled, he knew he had won the battle. "So I stood up, walked over to the cabin, and put my rifle inside, and then went over and watched the Indians working," said Ardill. In a few minutes, friendly words were exchanged and the crisis was over.

Time went by fast and season followed season. There was always something to do—land to break, fences to build, crops to plant, and animals to feed. The only machinery Ardill had was a plough and a mechanical seeder, so farming was a hard, slow job. But game was plentiful and the future looked good.

"The mosquitoes were the worst pests," said Ardill. "When I broke the land I used to get up at three a.m. and work until ten a.m. and then quit, because the mosquitoes were so bad. I worked again from eight to ten p.m. and then made a smudge [fire] to protect the horses, and hoped the day and the work was done."

When the family went to Hudson Hope in summer, they traveled at night to avoid the mosquitoes. There was no road for the twenty-mile trip, and the only transportation was a river boat or pack horses along an old Indian trail. In winter, the journey could be made by sleigh over the river ice, but Ardill never attempted it alone.

"A neighbor always used to go with me," he said. "I'd take two horses and a sleigh and he'd do the same, and we'd double up on the rough parts. The ice was never safe, you see, and if a horse went through, there had to be two of you to get him out. You wouldn't have had a chance on your own. The Peace made a dandy highway, but it was always dangerous, and many good teams were lost under its ice. Even at forty below there were many large holes in the ice, and you had to be careful to break trail in the snow not too close to the bank, where springs came into the river and the ice was very thin. These trips were very cold and we often ended up with frozen faces. The round trip to Hudson Hope took a week to ten days and you had to leave your wife at home alone to do the milking, so you didn't do it too often."

Hudson Hope was a mere hop, skip and jump compared to the 130-mile journey over land and river ice to Pouce Coupe that Ardill had to make to bring in seed grain. Another homesteader joined him on this trip and the men made about twenty miles a day, camping out along the way. When Ardill had to buy heavy equipment in Hudson Hope in summer, he would hitch up his team to the stone boat and drive off down the forest trail, stopping every so often to cut some trees to widen the path. Several creeks had to be forded or, when the water was high, the horses had to be swum across. Apart from trips to town, the only news came from the mailman, who traveled the trail once a month.

"Victoria was a long way off and maybe hadn't heard of the Peace River district," said Ardill. "So a small, forgotten part of B.C. rested in peace. Little by little we progressed and made a fair living. Each year we cleared and broke a few more acres and the log cabin had one addition after another to accommodate a growing family."

John was joined by a sister, Betty, and then two brothers, Dick and Tom. John and Dick still work on the ranch. Tom works with a firm of heavy equipment manufacturers near Fort St. John. Betty is married to a rancher and lives in Hudson Hope.

The family was not the only part of the Ardill ranch that expanded rapidly. The original cow and calf that Ardill bought in 1920 had multiplied by 1972 into some five hundred head of cattle. "Last year, we bought about twenty cattle, but until then we never bought any—they were all descended from our first cow and calf," he said.

As for land, the original homestead grant gradually turned into a spread that stretched for miles along the river bank and up into the distant hills.

A glimpse of Ardill family life in the late 1920s is contained in *Canyons, Cans and Caravans*, a book written by Eva Hassell, an English missionary who plodded through the Peace River country organizing a Sunday school by mail service. She reported that there were 3,000 people (and only one doctor) in the whole of the Peace River Block in 1928. In that year a sudden influx of 1,200 more settlers arrived, because at a Chicago international show the previous year, a prize for the best wheat and oats in the world had been won by a Peace River farmer.

Eva Hassell and another English woman, Iris Sayle, met the Ardills during a sixty-mile walk beside the river from Fort St. John to Hudson Hope, visiting the families which were scattered from seven to seventeen miles apart along the northern bank. They were delighted by the welcome and food they were given at the Ardills' cabin. "Mr. Ardill had just shot a moose and we found the meat delicious," wrote Miss Hassell. "They were delighted to hear that their four children could have Sunday school lessons by post. Both of them missed church services and sacraments and were particularly grieved that there had been no clergyman up the pack trail since any of their children were born. Indeed, as far as I could gather, no ordained clergyman had ever been up the trail at all."

Miss Hassell, who was also campaigning for a hospital in the area, said Mrs. Ardill's experiences were proof of the need for one. "Just before one baby was born, she went a hundred miles into Pouce Coupe to hospital in a sleigh, along the river for the first part of the way," wrote Miss Hassell. "Up the steep river banks the snow had melted and then frozen, and the sleigh turned over twice and she had to jump out."

Miss Hassell reported that Ardill had been unable to get in a threshing machine due to transportation problems, so he kept cows and pigs because they could be sent out by boat. "The farm was beautifully situated, and neither Mr. nor Mrs. Ardill would like to live anywhere else," she wrote. "The first thing we did was to help them put on the roof of their house, which had blown off in last night's storm. Mrs. Ardill said her sister in Brussels would be surprised to learn that this operation could be performed between tea and supper."

By the 1930s, the Ardills' isolation was decreasing and their prosperity was increasing. The children took their schooling by correspondence. As they grew bigger, so did the family cabin, eventually becoming sixty feet long. In 1940 the old cabin was finally replaced by the present house, built on almost the same location.

For twenty-six years, until 1956, the Ardill home was also the Farrell Creek post office and people from miles around picked up their mail in the family kitchen. Collecting the mail was the social event of the week for many homesteaders. In 1932 the road between Fort St. John and Hudson Hope was started, and Ardill and his son John took a team of horses and helped with the construction. The government allowed homeowners to work on the road in lieu of paying taxes. The work progressed slowly and it was not until about 1936 that the first car jolted along the road. In the same year, a bridge was put over Halfway River, a tributary of the Peace, to replace an old cable and hanging basket arrangement which had often proved a hair-raising way of getting from one side of the water to the other.

As cars and trucks took over from sleighs and pack horses, the original homesteaders no longer had their Peace River to themselves. Tourists were often hunters who did not have as much respect or need for the game as the farmers.

"In the old days there were sometimes sixty deer in our garden at one time," said Ardill. "They used to come right up to the house and my wife made pets of them. Now you don't see anything like that number. People shoot them from the road when they are on our property. Once someone shot a deer while Mrs. Ardill and our daughter were working in the garden—the bullet could easily have hit them instead of the animal."

As well as working on the ranch now that his father is dead, John Ardill also runs a trap line and a guiding business. He, too, dislikes the greedy hunter. "One bad winter recently the moose came down from the hills to feed and people shot them from their cars in the road," he said. "There were fifteen dead moose lying out there along the road and the snowplow plowed the bodies into the snowbanks. When the snow melted the stench was awful. People can be so bad."

Unless the provincial government shortens the hunting season and tightens the game regulations, John Ardill is afraid the moose and deer will vanish, as the elk and buffalo already have. He has dug up the skulls of many elk and buffalo on the ranch, but it is years since these animals were seen in the Peace River country.

Jack Ardill described it this way: "It used to be the land of the Peace, but there's no peace here now. We called them the good old days and that's what they were. They are long gone now, but it was good to have lived in them. Today the game is going like the buffalo—never to return. And that's what people call progress."

Chapter 5
Eugene Peterson
Prospector

The town of Sandon was the one-time silver capital of the Kootenays; now it is almost deserted. Eugene Peterson lives alone in the town, but it doesn't bother him. He has lived there since 1923, arriving when he was about six. And in those years he has seen Sandon smashed by two floods and disintegrate into one of the most romantic and picturesque ghost towns in B.C.

Sandon was doomed to disaster from the moment it came into existence, because of its crazy location. The town is situated on a creek in a steep and narrow mountain valley of the Slocan range, about twenty-two miles west of Kaslo in the West Kootenay. Landslides in the summer and avalanches in the winter have smashed into the isolated community almost every year. In winter the snowfall is so great that the fire hydrants had to be six feet high to prevent them being lost from sight under drifts. And even in summer the place gets less than its fair share of sunshine, because the mountains block out the sun from the valley for many hours a day. Sandon is wedged into a crack between two mountains, and the three miles of gravel linking it to the New Denver-Kaslo road are lined with trees that almost touch overhead. It is a gloomy, mysterious place.

Peterson is known as the mayor of Sandon and he enjoys the title, though he did not seek it. A bachelor, he lives in a neat and pretty little house amidst the broken and empty remains of a once-busy community.

"Like a lot of old-timers, I didn't like it here at first, but now I don't want to move," he said with a faint trace of Norwegian accent. "Now I'm working with some people to try to persuade the provincial government to preserve the town—not reconstruct it except, maybe, for a few buildings. But we want to stop the deterioration and save the buildings from getting any worse. We want to preserve the atmosphere of the place because this is a historic site."

Peterson was right. Sandon was the soul of the "Silvery South Slocan"—as the miners liked to call it—for more than half a century. Fortunes were made here by some people, but the vast majority of the miners lived only on dreams.

A miner named Eli Carpenter and his partner discovered the first ore in the area in October 1891. News of the strike must have spread far and fast, because it was a Virginian, Johnny Harris, who founded the town in 1892. He was among the first of that often notorious breed—real estate developers—and when he heard of the West Kootenay discovery he knew that hordes of men would soon be on their way. Harris laid out the town and later became the owner of two successful local mines, two hotels,

Eugene Peterson
77

several business blocks, and a livery stable.

"The town was named after a prospector, John Sandon," explained Peterson. By 1898, Sandon was a brawling, bustling city with a population of over two thousand, plus twenty-four hotels, twenty-three saloons, an opera house, brewery, cigar factory, two newspapers, and a red light district that was home to 115 ladies of easy virtue.

The silver-lead-zinc in the surrounding hills attracted miners because it was easily and cheaply mined. Scores of mines were scattered through the mountains, and Sandon was the boom town at the center of the action. Silver was king and there were so many men, mules and horses in Sandon that newcomers had to fight their way into town.

The mines in some cases were bolted, cemented, and even cabled to the sheer slopes overlooking the town. Tramlines carried ore buckets of galena to the belching mills below. After the galena had been smelted and the lead and silver extracted (zinc was often thrown away in those days), the metal went off to the world markets.

The community had its first setback in 1900, when a fire gutted the town's business section. Only Harris's livery stable was left intact. Rumor had it that the blaze started in a dressing room at the opera house, where a play called, ironically, "The Bitter Atonement"was being performed.

But a city that had become the capital of a vast silver empire was not easily wiped out. Three sawmills went into action immediately at rebuilding, and the very day after the fire, men were seen playing blackjack and stud poker on tables set up in the still-smoldering rubble. The whole town was rebuilt within months and Harris converted his livery stable into a hotel. The twenty-five room Reco became the pride of the community and numbered among its guests the mining elite of the 1900s. Harris and his wife operated the hotel continuously until his death in 1953.

The rebuilding of the town included construction of Sandon's most talked-about structure, the boardwalk over Carpenter Creek. By a strange twist of fate, this famous boardwalk was involved in the town's ultimate destruction. It came about this way.

Carpenter Creek runs through the center of the community and was originally crisscrossed by a series of intricate but inconvenient bridges. Unusual weather conditions can turn the normally quiet creek into a raging torrent in a matter of hours. In the enthusiasm of reconstruction after the fire, the townsfolk flumed the unpredictable creek and built a massive boardwalk right over the top of it. This structure became the town's main street and was the talk of all B.C.'s mining towns. In fact, Sandon was the only city in the world with a main street over a creek. The boardwalk was trodden with equal indifference by horses drawing ore wagons and by elegantly dressed women. But in 1955, Carpenter Creek burst through the boardwalk during spring runoff and smashed everything in its path. It was the death blow to the town which, like a cat, had had many lives in its sixty-three-year history.

About two thousand people were still living in Sandon when Peterson arrived there with his parents and brothers and sisters in the early 1920s. "I didn't like it at first, because it was so bare and rocky compared to what I'd been used to in Norway," he said. "There was hardly any grass then, because there were so many horses around to eat the grass.

"I guess there were two hundred horses when we came here, but in the early days before the railroad was built, there must have been eight hundred or nine hundred horses. People used horses for everything then, and they worked their hearts out up in those mountains. You could see their bones all over the hills when I was a youngster and in some cases they really had been worked to death.

"As kids we used to roam the hills all summer visiting the different mines and never even thinking about bears," he said. "There were mining camps all over the hills and lots of individual prospectors living in cabins by themselves. They always welcomed us kids, and the cooks in the mining

Eugene Peterson
79

camps were especially good to us. In wintertime we'd be out on skis all the time and we'd have great rides back to town. The trails would drop about three thousand feet in four miles, and we were on our skis all day. In winter I would not even go downtown without putting my skis on."

The whole countryside was mining mad when Peterson was a boy and he absorbed everything he heard and saw—from techniques to tall tales. "Old-timers told me it was the cheapest country to go mining in, because of the ore outcroppings," he said. "But there aren't any outcroppings left now, because the country's been gone over with a fine tooth comb by some of the very best prospectors. You didn't need a lot of expensive equipment either—just a pick, shovel, wheelbarrow and some packhorses to bring it out. Some packhorse owners would stake you if they thought you were on to a good thing."

Peterson was continually astonished by the grim determination that kept so many men returning to the mountains even though they seldom had any luck. "I still don't know why some of the old-timers did it," he said. "You could follow their trails for miles up into the hills—good trails through really rough country, with bridges across the canyons. You would find their cabins way above timberline—very well-built cabins, but hardly any work done on the mine. I guess they felt good up there, that's why they did it. They were young men when they started and they went back year after year."

Peterson said many of the old miners lived year round on their claims and only came into Sandon for essential supplies. They would stay in the hills until they were so old they were forced to come out.

"I remember meeting one old fellow of about eighty in the middle of winter when the snow was deep," he recalled. "He was going up a trail to his mine and he had such a sore back that he was stooped over. I asked him if he was working his claim, and he looked up to where his mine was and said, 'I'm driving a tunnel in up there and if I have to I'll drive it right through the mountain,' and his eyes shone and I was amazed, because I thought he was on his last legs.

"He surprised us all, that old fellow did. He drove a lot of tunnel all by himself for the next couple of years, and his back improved too. He slugged away up there doing everything by hand. He drilled and mucked and blasted and trailed all the muck out. But he had no ore—he was just looking. Then he went out to visit his daughter in Rossland one Christmas and caught a bug from civilization and died of pneumonia."

Winter was the best time for moving heavy equipment, because it was easier to haul by sleigh than by wagon on the steep trails. First, one horse would be sent down the trail with a drag behind it to pack the snow. Then two horses would be driven down to widen it further, and eventually the trail would have been broadened into a road.

"That's the way they hauled up enormous pieces of machinery weighing many tons that they could not even have moved in summertime," said Peterson. "They brought up a huge air compressor to a mine called the Ivanhoe over the snow that way. But later on during the summer, a very heavy part of the compressor broke down and they had to send out for a replacement. This piece of machinery weighed far more than any horse was able to carry, but they were determined to get it up there."

The miners evolved a plan of action that called for the services of a strong mule and six of the strongest men who would volunteer. "It was really ironic that they picked the best mule they could find as the sacrifice animal," he said. "Then they went downtown and loaded this great big hunk of metal onto the mule and headed for the mine. Every time the mule got tired, the six men leaned up against the mule and tried to take the weight off him so that the mule could rest. But the mule got terrible tired, and in the high altitude of the mountain it was even harder for him. When they got to the mine, they took off the load and the mule just fell down and died."

Eugene Peterson
81

What a miner always feared was an accident when he was alone in the mountains and miles away from help. Peterson remembered one old man who fell and broke his leg when he was working his claim by himself. "He lay in his tent for two weeks, but no one came, so he made himself a splint and some crutches and hobbled down the mountain for five miles," he said. "His leg healed—it wasn't perfect, but it healed."

When Peterson was a boy, there were forty or fifty producing mines in the Sandon area, but only about a dozen were major producers. Each person was only allowed one claim at a time, so there were always a lot of miners around. And there was an unwritten rule among the prospectors of not snooping around each other's claim.

"In fact, it was a law-abiding community because there were so many Americans here who did not like the lawlessness of the States at that time and they were determined it wasn't going to be repeated in B.C.," said Peterson. "I only remember one murder in all that time—a fellow got shot after a drinking party.

"There was always money around, because you could usually sell a claim for five hundred dollars. That seemed to be the magic figure, I don't know why. Of course, you would get more if it was really good, but five hundred dollars was the usual figure."

As a boy, Peterson remembered being told that nowhere in the world were there so many mines in such a small area as there were around Sandon. "It was a pretty busy place when I was growing up and Sandon was well past its heyday then," he recalled. "There were still four or five hotels and several fairly big boarding houses, and the train came up here three days a week."

Sandon was served by two railroads in its early days and that is a story in itself. The first was the Kaslo and Slocan (known as the K & S), a narrow-gauge line pushed into Sandon by the Great Northern Railway Company. It carried passengers and ore out to Kaslo, and eventually forty-five miles south to Nelson, where it continued to Spokane and other points in the U.S. The second was the Canadian Pacific Railway, which sent one of its octopus tentacles south from Revelstoke into Sandon on a 4.5 per cent grade, the steepest in the world at that time.

Sandon was not big enough to hold two such fierce rivals, and a price war broke out between them. The war was not restricted to economics for long. On one memorable day, some daring employees of the K & S staged a spectacular attack on their mammoth rival. They backed one of their steam engines close to the CPR station, tied cables around it, wrenched it off its foundations, and dumped it into the creek. But inevitably the CPR won the war. The K & S went bankrupt and ceased operations in 1910, while the CPR continued running into Sandon until the flood of 1955.

By 1920, a combination of strikes and falling market prices for lead and silver began closing the mines. Silver had been bullish in earlier days because the U.S. government had seriously considered going off the gold standard in favor of silver. However, that possibility never became a reality, and Sandon suffered as a result. The Depression brought even tougher times and the storekeepers suffered as well as the miners.

As a teenager in the Depression, Peterson worked as a store clerk to make a little extra cash for his family. And the experience left him with some searing memories. "I remember an old-timer called Mickey who had been looking for ore for many, many years and the storekeeper had faith in him," said Peterson. "Mickey wasn't a drinker—he was sober all the time I knew him—and by 1930 the storekeeper had grubstaked him for food and supplies so long that his bill was seven thousand dollars."

The storekeeper, Johnny Black, never got his money back; he died while Mickey was still looking for his fortune. The old prospector assumed that Black's daughter, who had inherited the store, would continue her father's largesse.

But she instructed young Peterson not to give Mickey any more credit, because she did not have enough money to buy anything herself. So it fell to the teenage clerk to tell Mickey that his credit was cut off. The problem was that the old prospector just ignored the news.

"It seemed like he hadn't heard me and he gave me a big order for dynamite and fuses and the carbide they had to have for their lamps," said Peterson. Time and again Mickey returned to the store, asking for the supplies he was sure would be waiting for him. Finally, he threw up his hands in despair and said to Peterson, "You've got to get that carbide, man, I'm working in the dark." He was in such a sad state that Peterson reached in his pocket and gave him fifty cents of his own money.

Peterson did not work at the store for long. He was succeeded by his brother who clerked for many years and went by the nickname "Snoose," a word meaning snuff. "He got the nickname because when he was a kid all the Scandinavian miners sitting around town on benches in the evening would give him money and send him to buy snoose for them," said Peterson. "He was buying so much snoose that the storekeeper started calling him that and the name stuck—it's still with him."

In 1933, Sandon experienced its first major flood; the upper end of the flume on Carpenter Creek became plugged with uprooted trees and boulders carried down by the rushing water. Buildings on trestles at the edge of the flume were severely undermined and in some cases totally destroyed.

"The 1933 flood wasn't nearly as bad as the one in 1955 and I know because I was here for them both," said Peterson. "But a woman drowned in the 1933 flood, and no one did in 1955. She was leaning on her clothes line—trying to save the clothes, I guess—and a fence gave way and she fell in. You'd never guess from the look of that creek now what it can look like when it's in flood."

Peterson was in his late teens when he met an old

prospector, Jack Wilson, who had a great effect on his life. "Wilson was probably the best friend I ever had and he taught me a great deal," said Peterson. "I spent many hours listening to him and I'll never forget him." The odd friendship between an old prospector down on his luck and a youth not long out of school meant a great deal to both of them.

"Wilson more or less adopted me," said Peterson. "Most of his money had gone when I met him, but he was still considered lucky. He'd made a strike at the end of the First World War and had made about seventy thousand dollars' profit in a short time, so he was considered what the miners used to call 'stakey.' But he'd spent it all by the time I met him.

"I've found out by checking on some things that he always told me the truth. He was one of those rare people who did not exaggerate about how much ore was somewhere. Usually when you went to take a look at some claim it was only about one-tenth the size—or it was much lower grade—than what you had been told about it.

'There's a tendency in all old-timers to exaggerate. I remember one claim I staked that had become available, and government records showed that the old-timers who had worked there twenty-five years previously had shipped out eight tons of ore. But when I met one of these old-timers, I asked him out of habit, 'How much ore did you get?' and he said he'd got a carload. Well, a carload meant forty tons. But Wilson didn't exaggerate like that.

"Old-timers have told me that Wilson was a regular daredevil, the way he drove six-horse teams down the mountain here, when he had a contract for many years to haul ore from the Slocan Star mine," said Peterson. "He came down the mountain, around all those switchbacks with a bunch of horses, and it was quite a sight, the old-timers told me.

"But a strange thing had happened to him when he got older, and when I knew him. He had lost his nerve and wasn't even able to drive one horse. He couldn't handle the most gentle horse we had here. He would always manage to get the horse nervous and he'd have trouble with it."

Wilson was prospecting, sometimes with a hired man working for him as a miner, during the last fifteen years of his life. "His money gradually eroded away, but, as long as I can remember, whenever he bought some clothing for himself he bought the same for me too. He always bought really good quality clothes, like wool flannel shirts."

Wilson was killed when he was working on road construction near Sandon and a rock rolled down a mountainside and smashed into him. "He was just about at the bottom of his savings when it happened," said Peterson.

Another old-timer who made a great impression on Peterson was Johnny Harris, the Virginian who developed Sandon and was a living tourist attraction by the time he died in 1953 at the age of eighty-nine. One of Harris's mines yielded silver valued at $200,000 during one week of operation, but most of his fortune came from real estate dealings.

"He never bothered to sweat and work his head off," said Peterson. "He made his money by sitting in his office, and luck always came his way right to the last. Somebody would turn something up for him—like when prospectors built a trail across his Reco ground and uncovered a rich vein, one of the richest in the whole camp. From the vein, I believe Johnny made about six hundred thousand dollars in a few years, and costs were small.

"There were excellent miners here, hand miners, so it didn't cost much money to have a crew of men working for you. And the ore was rich and easy to get. That's how Johnny Harris got his start and then he branched out into real estate." The real estate included two hotels, several business blocks, and a livery stable.

But Harris's fortune had almost slipped away by the time he became old, and he was not strong enough to hike into his claims any more.

"It was a routine of his that whenever the snow got deep every winter, he would pull out all his claim papers and review them—it seemed to give him a psychological boost," said Peterson. "He would say that as long as he didn't sell the Reco Hotel he would be okay. In his mind he was still a millionaire. He believed he had a fortune in claims, if he could only get to them."

One day Peterson heard Harris boasting to a newcomer that he was the best poker player in the country, because his eyesight was so good he could see right through a deck of cards. "Well, I was walking by at the time and heard Johnny say this, so I stopped and reached for a deck of cards close by and was about to say, 'Let's see you do it, Johnny,' but he realized right away what I was going to do," said Peterson. "So he turned to the stranger and said that after he had flu last winter his eyes had not been so good and he couldn't do the trick anymore."

Peterson had turned to prospecting when his dream of agricultural college came to nothing. He prospected all over B.C., sometimes with a partner, but often alone.

"I've sometimes been alone in the hills for a month or so and no one knew where I was," he said. "In circumstances like that a guy could easily have an accident and die, and his body would never be found. But I always carried a rifle and treated grizzlies with respect. I never did work for other people as a miner, only for myself. I hate the thought of working for anyone else—I think I'd rather go and pick apples instead."

The Second World War created a tremendous demand for minerals like tin and tungsten, which is used as an alloy of steel. Peterson was exempted from military service to look for minerals and had his best luck in the Salmo-Creston area.

"Tin used to come from countries like Malaysia and when the Japanese cut off those supplies from the allies, there was a desperate need to find a source of priority war minerals at home," said Peterson. "My prospecting work

Eugene Peterson

was considered so important that I could get things that other people couldn't. For instance, the manager of Cominco couldn't get tires for his car and I could, and he didn't like that much."

Peterson's wartime hunt for minerals did not begin auspiciously, because he and his partner, Joe Gallow, a well-known prospector in the Sandon area for years, were both broke.

"We each had to borrow a hundred dollars from friends to finance our expedition and that was the only time I ever borrowed money," said Peterson. "But we struck ore that gave us five thousand dollars in two weeks. That's the way it goes. Sometimes you'll strike something that gives you a thousand dollars a day for several weeks and then the ore will peter out to nothing, and you'll go six or seven years before you find anything again."

Peterson and his partner took the advice of a mining engineer and started prospecting beside an old mine near Salmo, where tungsten ore had been found previously. The tip paid off. Within two weeks they found tungsten ore on land that was owned by Cominco Ltd.

"It was very rich on the ground, and promising," said Peterson. The two prospectors went to see a Cominco executive, whom Gallow knew personally, and they reached swift agreement.

"We laid our cards on the table and trusted him and he gave us what we thought was a real good deal," said Peterson. "Cominco paid us five thousand dollars cash and gave us a ten per cent interest in the whole deal. So though we'd started out with nothing, we had five thousand dollars within two weeks."

But when Cominco started digging into the ore, they discovered that the twenty-four foot wide surface strip did not represent the real width of the ore. The ore was actually only about eight feet wide, because limestone had eroded away one side of it and the slab had broken and tipped upward.

It had lain on the mountainside for a million years until it looked like it was the width of the vein, explained Peterson. "The rich ore was all that was exposed and it was very deceiving, so when they dug through it and found the ore wasn't as wide or as rich as it looked, the whole thing was abandoned." It was a bitter blow for Peterson who desperately wanted to help the war effort, but he refused to give up, and spent the rest of the war hunting for minerals with varying success.

He and Gallow staked a large group of claims on Sheep Creek, a tributary of the Salmo River, and these claims were attractive enough to persuade the Bralorne mining outfit to pay $2,000 for an option on them.

Next summer, when Peterson was working in the same area, he followed a game trail that went right through the middle of the claims—a route he had taken many times before. On the trail was a big rock, just like a step, that everyone who followed the trail had to walk on.

"I knew the rock was a piece of tungsten ore, but it was loose, and I figured it could have come from miles away," he said. "I hadn't even bothered to put the ultra-violet light on it to see how rich it was, because I took it for granted that the mining engineers working for Bralorne, and perhaps even my partner, had looked at it."

Peterson explained the method of testing ore was to put a thick black velvet cloth on top of the outcrop, place an ultra-violet lamp under it, and then examine the rock. If the rock was tungsten, it would give off a blue-white fluorescence.

Peterson asked Gallow if he had bothered to put a lamp on the big rock, and the answer was no. "He didn't even know it was there—he acted surprised," said Peterson. "So we walked up the trail and put the lamp on it and it was much richer than the other ore we had seen up there. Immediately we got excited, because we'd been wondering if we could interest someone in these claims."

Eugene Peterson
89

The immediate task, however, was to find out where the rock had come from, so Peterson and Gallow took off in different directions to search the mountain.

"In no time at all I found myself in a formation that was completely unfavorable for what we call contact metamorphic deposits, so I stopped to puzzle over the problem," said Peterson. "I thought that if I kept going up the mountain, I would be too far away. Besides, I'd been up there many times and hadn't seen anything. So I decided to go back down to the rock and take a look at it again, and see if I could come up with some other direction to go in. So I stood right on top of that piece of ore and looked down the mountain, through the jack pine, and about a hundred or a hundred and fifty feet below me I could see what looked like an outcrop.

"Outcrops are always interesting in the timber and overburden, because there weren't too many of them there. So I decided to go down and see what sort of formation it was. And when I got there, I found it was the ore body. I guess that piece of rock I'd found first had been on the top end of the ore body and had rolled.

"So I called to my partner—he was busy knocking samples off—and he came back down. The brush was so thick that you couldn't walk through it to trace the ore around the mountain. So I ended up crawling on my hands and knees through the alders in the direction of the outcrop, between the granite and limestone. And in about a hundred yards, I found another outcrop. That was all we needed. We went back to Cominco and they took an option on it."

Unfortunately this story, like so many mining anecdotes, ended up as a tale of frustration. Cominco had just started work on Peterson's discovery when a mine in Idaho, where the company was mining stibnite, suddenly ran into the richest tungsten ore in the country.

"It was so much richer than anything up here that they were able to shovel it up and supply all the demands of the allies," said Peterson. "Immediately the high priority fell off our tungsten ore in Canada and we just had to forget it. Cominco dropped our claims, and we dropped them.

"We gave everything to the fellow who had owned the two key claims originally. We told him he could have the whole works, and walked out on it. But, as luck would have it, he made money out of it a few years later. The mine in Idaho didn't last very long and they started up the other tungsten mines again. So that fellow we gave the claims to made a little money out of them. That's the way it goes in mining.

"A lot of outcroppings look good, but they suddenly end. It happens all the time. That's why companies diamond drill when they can; they strip with bulldozers and send in geologists. In those days I wasn't much interested in geology, other than where there was ore. I can still remember how impatient I got with a geological engineer who kept stopping and looking at the depth of rocks. But now I can see why geologists do that. It's all part of the picture."

Peterson said only a few people made really big fortunes in the Sandon area, and probably the largest, around ten million dollars, was piled up by a couple named George and Viola MacMillan. In 1948 the MacMillans took over the Victor Mine, an old silver-lead-zinc property originally discovered in 1922 by Mrs. George Petty of Sandon.

According to Peterson, Mrs. Petty was a very tough woman, six feet tall, and as capable of digging pits as her husband. "She used to come to town in britches and high boots with a big pack sack," he said. "She was always potting bears—she wasn't afraid of them at all."

One summer day, Mrs. Petty's husband became ill from the heat and had to go home to bed. While he was recuperating, his wife continued working in the mine ditch and found the first trace of the ore that eventually became worth a fortune. The couple mined the ore for as long as they could, but when age caught up with them, the property was worked on a lease basis by a man named Ernest Doney and his family.

For eighteen years the Doney family worked the mine, doing well out of it and shipping the ore to the Trail smelter. Then, in 1948, along came Mrs. MacMillan, president of a company which she and her husband called ViolaMac, and paid $65,000 for the Victor property.

Until the MacMillans bought the mine, all work on the Victor had been done by hand mining methods. The narrow, high-grade vein on a slope of Queen Bess Mountain near Sandon had been opened on five levels.

"But, as it turned out, Doney had been working on the very top of the ore and didn't know there was so much there," said Peterson. "He had driven a cross-cut from the lowest tunnel and it had missed the vein. This cross-cut tunnel got smaller and smaller, until you had to get down on your hands and knees to move forward. Doney eventually had to put the muck in what we call a powder box and pull it out with a rope to where he had a car and track."

Peterson was sure that Doney gave up only because the tunnel was so small and uncomfortable. MacMillan, however, was convinced there must be a substantial body of ore in the mine, even though many little faults in the rock kept slicing through the veins.

"But even MacMillan started to get a little worried after a while, and so he decided to try to find a lower vein," said Peterson. "So he and his men drove another cross-cut, different from the one driven by Doney that was so small. Then they swung the main tunnel slowly around in that direction. And after driving only a few feet, they struck this large ore body that eventually netted them profits of about ten million dollars or more. The total production was nearly fifteen million dollars.

"And when they drove back on the vein, Doney's tunnel was within six inches of it. Doney was working there as a foreman at the time, and they say he just stood there for the longest time looking at the hole they'd exposed, and realizing how close he had been."

Production from the mine then became so enormous that the Chicago *Tribune* sent a reporter to take a look at the property in 1953, and he wrote that it was returning a million dollars' profit every year.

The Chicago journalist was fascinated by Mrs. Mac-Millan who, at that time, spent ten months of the year at the mine with only brief trips to Toronto, where she owned a large, expensive home. He wrote:

> Perhaps remembering that she had walked over a good part of Canada before she struck it rich, Mrs. MacMillan watches over her property with all the attention that a hen gives its brood. On most days she can be seen standing at the entrance to the ViolaMac base metal mine, her own private Fort Knox, which projects from a mountainside nearly five thousand feet above a remote valley. It is one of the biggest silver-lead-zinc producers in Canada.
>
> Mrs. MacMillan's daily routine parallels that of her miners. She lives in a decrepit, one-room shack near the mineshaft and takes her meals in the camp cookhouse with the hired help. A small, attractive woman, nearing fifty, she handles a diamond drill or pick with the best of them and often teaches novice miners the tricks of the trade.

The Chicago reporter described how Mrs. MacMillan, who became one of the richest women in Canada, started life as the daughter of an Ontario farmer. In 1924, she met and married George MacMillan, the son of a prospector, and opened a boarding house in Windsor, Ontario, to help her husband who was struggling along as a junior stockbroker.

Through reading material her husband brought home, Mrs. MacMillan developed an interest in mining and eventually convinced her husband to quit his job and join her in a search for gold.

For two decades the MacMillans scraped and saved every nugget they could find without hitting anything like a big strike. Finally, in 1944, they quit the gold fields of Quebec, northern Ontario, and the Northwest Territories and turned their attention to the newly-developed base metals field in interior B.C.

But the sledding was tough in B.C. too and for two years the MacMillans were hard pressed to clear even the ten dollars a day that prospectors consider the minimum required to maintain self respect.

Then, just as the MacMillans were considering a retreat to the boarding house business in the late 1940s, they learned that the Victor was for sale. Mrs. MacMillan was convinced the mine was well worth buying, but she didn't have the $65,000 asking price, of which $45,000 had to be cash.

"So, I just floated some stock to raise it," she told the Chicago reporter years later. Eventually, she bought out the stock with profits from the mine and the MacMillans' success story was complete.

Clarence Cunningham was another of the few men who made big money out of the Sandon area mines, but Peterson remembered him more for his kindness than his money.

"He came in here during the latter part of the First World War and took an option on the Queen Bess mine," he recalled. "This mine had been moderately successful, but the known ore bodies had been mined out and the place was lying dormant. So Cunningham got a lease on it and, after driving only a very short distance, he struck an ore body that in less than a year turned out to be the easiest ore to mine in the whole Slocan.

"Cunningham took out a million dollars' worth of ore in a year and not many mines here have succeeded in taking out that much in a year. After he made his fortune at Queen Bess, he constructed a sort of little empire in the valley right on Carpenter Creek. He put up a big concentrator to concentrate ore from many other mines that he had developed. And he built himself a palatial home, the biggest and finest in the Slocan area."

But, like so many early mining magnates, Cunningham did not hold onto his money. He took over many mines in the Slocan area and at one time was the largest mining operator in the Kootenays. However, the expense of building the huge concentrator combined with declining metal prices and the Depression eventually swallowed up his fortune.

"He was actually deeply in debt to the banks when he died in the late 1930s," said Peterson. "But the banks didn't foreclose on him as long as he was alive, because they had faith that he could pull through. It was sort of a gentleman's agreement. And Cunningham always had the appearance of having money. As long as he owned these million-dollar claims, he felt he was still a millionaire. And at the last he wasn't even solvent.

"I remember Cunningham as a very fine man. When we were youngsters, and even after we'd grown up, we would go by his home when we were out hunting and he would always invite us in. He had a cook and there was always lots to eat in his house even in the hungry thirties. He would insist that we come in and have a meal whenever we went by his place. And he was just the same when he was up in the mountains. It didn't matter where you met him—he was a real fine fellow."

Peterson did not spend all his life prospecting. For many years he worked through the winter in the Sandon power plant and then headed into the mountains as soon as summer arrived. He was very proud of Sandon's history of power production because it dated back such a long way. Johnny Harris founded the original Sandon Water and Light Company and it started operating in the mid-1890s, only two months after the plant in Nelson which had the first generator in B.C.

"But I'm sure Sandon can claim the distinction of being the first town in B.C. to be serviced by electricity," said Peterson. "Nelson's generator was so small it couldn't possibly have served a whole town anywhere near the size of Sandon at that time.

"Our power is now produced from what might be one of the oldest generators in B.C. It comes from the old Silversmith mine and it was installed in the plant in 1916 or 1918. I believe it was originally the first generator ever owned by the city of Vernon."

Not only was Sandon well serviced by power much earlier than most of B.C., but it also had excellent fire fighting equipment in the form of high-pressure hydrants. These were the famous six feet high hydrants that stood out even in deep snow.

"They provided very high-pressure water and there's only two left in town now," said Peterson. "I keep an eye on them, otherwise they'd have been dug up long ago. We keep water running out of them to show that they are still in use, but we still have to chase away guys who want to take them as souvenirs."

Peterson said he never married. "Most of us prospectors were always running away from a woman, or else there were none around," he joked. So, with his relatives dead or living in distant parts, Peterson lived on alone in what used to be the family home and worked as a custom miner for a big company.

He had neighbors for a few years during the Second World War when about 1,000 Japanese-Canadians were interned in Sandon in a now-controversial security measure. But in 1945 they left, and the miner was alone again.

The well-kept, white-painted Peterson house was one of the few to survive the big flood, because it was located in the only part of town where the creek did not overflow its banks.

"Sure, I was here in the flood of 1955," said Peterson. "There had been several days of very high temperatures—up into the nineties—just before it happened. And the snowpack the previous winter had been much bigger than usual, so the runoff was heavy."

A flash thunderstorm during a sultry June day was all that was needed to transform usually docile Carpenter Creek into a deadly torrent. "It was the only time I can remember when the sky went yellow," said Peterson. "Then came this terrific thunderstorm and the noise of the creek was so loud you couldn't even hear the thunder, although you could see the lightning flashing all around. It was as bright as day when the lightning flashed, but in between flashes it was pitch black, because the power plant went out."

It was a night of terror for the eleven or so families still living in Sandon at the time. "The creek took out most of the town in just a few hours. The noise was terrific. Huge trees and boulders five feet across came crashing down the creek and we worked for about forty-eight hours without sleep to keep the water back. By the light of the storm, I watched the houses and hotels being undermined and toppling into the creek—one building maybe a hundred feet long fell into the creek in minutes.

"I remember only one guy got drunk and he spent the night ferrying the lady bootlegger back and forth across the creek. When she got to one side she decided she wanted to go back to the other side, and every time he carried her she would reward him with something to drink. Next day, everything was covered with mud. There was really nothing left to salvage—it was all gone and no one could ever find it."

When the waters receded, most of the town had been swept away. There were twenty-nine washouts on the nine-mile CPR branch line, and the section foreman became a man without a train or a station. One CPR building in Sandon was overturned and the station was washed from

Eugene Peterson
97

its foundation and left at a crazy angle. The line was promptly closed, and most of the few remaining families fled with the railway. Except, of course, for Peterson and Johnny Harris's widow. Mrs. Harris lived on into the 1960s, occupying a neat, tidy suite in the back of the Virginia block, one of the few survivors of the flood. Finally, there was only Peterson left. If it had not been for the arrival of occasional young settlers, and looters ripping apart the old buildings as the mania for historical things boomed, the town would have died completely.

The young people proved a great asset to Sandon as they repaired some of the old houses. Peterson treated them with amused tolerance, offering friendly advice and lending tools to the constant stream of callers.

The looters, slowly at first but more quickly as word spread, systematically tore their way through the ghost town, carrying away everything that could be moved. One woman took out nearly two box car loads to Indiana. Men in search of money almost destroyed the six-hundred-pound door of the old bank vault in their efforts to open it. No one knows what they found inside, but the smashed door was left to rust.

A valiant effort was made in the early 1970s by magazine publisher Bill Barlee to buy and restore the town. But the effort failed, as did a subsequent attempt to enlist aid from the provincial government.

"I'd like to see the town kept the way it is, with the tourists under much closer supervision," said Peterson. "Thousands of visitors come here every summer and they keep me away from my work for as much as four hours a day with all the questions they ask."

But for most of the year, Sandon is as quiet as a ghost town should be. The mines have long been abandoned and the headframes stand silent, blistering in the sun, while the picks and shovels of the miners rust in the undergrowth. Most of the buildings are rotting shells, and the timbers of the old boardwalk are smashed like matchsticks amongst the boulders of the creek. There are still a few glimpses of the town as it used to be. There is the date 1900 written outside the old city hall. And a door marked "Sandon Public School" stands high and dry above the creek, leading nowhere.

Peterson is not at all a gloomy man. But as he looked out over the ruins of the once-bustling town where he has spent his adult life, he became wistful.

"I could have been a millionaire by now . . . but the outcroppings petered out," he said.

Chapter 6
Bob Middleton
Manager
of a Hudson's Bay Post

All the retired Hudson's Bay Company managers now living in British Columbia have a story to tell. In the early part of the century, their lonely posts were far more than stores; they were everything from community centers to first aid clinics.

Bob Middleton of McLeod Lake was one of those post managers, and many of his experiences were typical of that now-vanished way of life, but it is for his other, unique experiences that his story is the one to be told. For example, he was the Hudson's Bay man who sold ammunition to Albert Johnson, the Mad Trapper of Rat River, and witnessed the start of Canada's greatest man hunt. His wife,

Nancy, adds a further dimension to their story because she is the daughter of the late Capt. Thomas Smellie, who commanded the Hudson's Bay northern supply ship *Nascopie* in the uncharted waters of the eastern Arctic for nearly thirty years.

The Middletons live in what for them is the deep south—McLeod Lake, about ninety miles north of Prince George. They are still running a store, but now it is their own rather than the Hudson's Bay's. People in many different parts of northern B.C. know and like them, for their community involvement has touched many lives. For miles up and down the John Hart Highway, a mention of the Middletons' names brings instant praise for their kindness and humanity.

The history of Canada is so tightly interwoven with the growth of the Hudson's Bay Company that it is sometimes hard to tell country from company. Middleton is one of an army of thousands of men and women who worked for the company during its more than three hundred years of history.

The saga of the Hudson's Bay Company started in 1670, when King Charles II granted a charter to the Governor and Company of Adventurers of England trading into Hudson's Bay. Under the terms of its charter the company was granted "the sole trade and commerce of all these seas, straits, bays, rivers, lakes, creeks and sounds, in whatsoever latitude they shall be, that lie within the entrance of the straits, commonly called Hudson's Straits, together with all the lands and territories upon the countries, coasts and confines of the seas, bays, lakes, rivers, creeks and sounds aforesaid." The charter must have been the most sweeping ever granted to any company.

The first trading post was established in 1668 on the east coast of James Bay and several more followed in the general area of James and Hudson bays. To these posts, goods were brought out annually by ship from England to be traded for furs with the Indians of Canada.

Bob Middleton
101

The trading posts gradually spread inland and westward across the prairies, and then fierce rivalry developed between the Hudson's Bay Company and the North West Company, spurring trading expansion into B.C. at the start of the nineteenth century.

Like so many Hudson's Bay Company employees, Middleton joined the company from Scotland and in 1925, crossed the Atlantic to become an apprentice clerk.

"I expected a land of snow and ice, but when I arrived it was in the middle of a beautiful summer," said Middleton. He was posted to Wabasca, Alberta, about fifty miles northeast of Lesser Slave Lake and two days on horseback from the railroad. Seven months later the company issued his first orders to move—the orders that came so often in the years ahead. Hudson's Bay employees had to be prepared to pack their bags frequently.

Middleton's first move took him to Fort St. John in northern B.C., where he stayed until 1929.

"It was a wee bit more primitive than where I had been living in Scotland," he admitted. "The hardest thing was getting up in the middle of the night to unload freight when it was forty or fifty below.

"The freight came in by horses from the railroad and we had to unload it as soon as it arrived, put it in a warehouse, and check it. But staff was no problem, because in those days, as well as the post manager, we had a bookkeeper, a junior clerk, a storekeeper, an outside man, and umpteen servants to do practically nothing. Today the same work is done by two men."

Soon Middleton was attending to far more than his clerical duties: he learned about fur buying, and when he went back to England for a holiday, he took a two-month course on the subject at the London warehouse.

"That was quite a help, because there weren't any books about fur at the time," he said. "But I guess I learned the most from my first post manager—he was very good and he taught me a lot. We used to have long haggles with some customers who knew a lot about prices. Of course, customers are more difficult to deal with now than they were in the old days, because today they expect the top price for everything. Better education, I think.

"The amount of fur coming into a store goes up and down because the animals go in cycles. One year you have an abundance of land animals and a scarcity of water animals. Then a few years later you'll have practically no land animals and an abundance of water animals, like muskrats and mink.

"Just before the stock market crash the company was paying very high prices. For instance, marten and mink were fetching enormous prices, sixty and sixty-five dollars, and silver fox would fetch one hundred dollars. Now you can buy the same thing for six to ten dollars. Silver foxes are farmed now, and the same thing with mink. Mink farms have more or less killed the price of wild mink, but I still think the wild mink is a better fur; it's just more colored."

The stock market crash in 1929 had a big effect on prices, and many post managers feared the Hudson's Bay Company might go out of business. "There were all kinds of rumors going around, and at one time we thought we'd end up working for the Americans," he said. "We heard the shareholders had to put more money in and it was just touch and go. That's when the company got away from all those servants around the place. That's when a post started to be a one-man operation instead of five men."

After several postings in the Northwest Territories, Middleton went to the far northern corner of the territory to become post manager at Fort McPherson on the Peel River, a tributary of the Mackenzie. The year was 1931, shortly before the manhunt for the Mad Trapper riveted Canadians to their radio sets every night for weeks.

The Mad Trapper called himself Albert Johnson, but his real identity is still a mystery. He rocked the country with his defiance of the RCMP in 1931-32.

Middleton's part in the drama began in the winter of

1931 when a stranger came into the post at Fort McPherson several times to buy ammunition and other supplies.

"I had him down as a criminal from the start," said Middleton. "While he was dealing with me over the counter he kept glancing over his shoulder as though he expected someone to come up behind him."

The stranger asked for both shotgun and rifle ammunition. When Middleton remarked, "You must be well equipped with guns," the man snarled in reply, "That's none of your business." He paid for his purchases from a large roll of bills.

Constable Edgar (Spike) Millen of the RCMP detachment at Arctic Red River, on the Mackenzie just south of Fort McPherson, was the Mountie who originally tried to check out the uncommunicative newcomer to the area. Millen had dinner with Middleton after a vain attempt to interview the stranger and recounted how the man had claimed to be Albert Johnson of Arctic Red River. When the Mountie told the trapper he was surprised because he thought he knew everyone in that settlement, Johnson replied: "That's my name and where I come from is none of your business."

Millen confided to Middleton: "I can't arrest him because we don't like him, but if he tries to trap without a licence I'll go after him. I have a feeling that he's going to give us some trouble." The remark was prophetic.

When the trapping season started, an Indian came into the post and complained to Middleton that Johnson had built a log cabin on the Rat River and was springing his traps.

"He said he'd reset his traps several times, but when he last patrolled his line the traps were hung up in trees," said Middleton. "He told me he knew the crazy man had done it, because he'd left footprints as big as snowshoes. So I advised him to go to Arctic Red River where the police were stationed, and that's what started the whole thing."

Constable Alfred King and Joe Bernard, an Indian

who served as a special constable and interpreter, set out from Arctic Red River to investigate. They traveled by dog team in a blinding snowstorm and stayed overnight at the Hudson's Bay post with Middleton, as was the custom of the time. On the morning of December 28, they went on to Johnson's cabin to check on his trapping licence and found that the cabin had been constructed like the block house of an old-style fort.

"It was built of double rows of big logs and just had little peepholes in it instead of windows," said Middleton. "And the trapper had constructed it partly underground by digging down about three feet with logs over the top, so he could stand and look out through these peepholes on all sides and shoot through them if he wanted to."

King tried for an hour to persuade the trapper to open the cabin door, but he refused, so the police decided to obtain a search warrant. They returned a week later with two more men, staying overnight again with Middleton because his post was a good half-way point on the journey.

On New Year's Eve King knocked on the trapper's cabin door for the second time and said, "Open in the name of the law." There was no reply. Then, as the constable raised his arm to smash the door with an axe, he was shot. He managed to crawl out of the line of fire, and his companions risked their lives to lash him to a sled while the trapper continued to fire. They did the eighty-mile trip to Aklavik in twenty hours with the temperature below zero all the time, and King's life was saved.

Inspector Alexander Eames, commander of the RCMP's Western Arctic sub-district, realized that he had a very nasty customer on his hands. He used an amateur radio station, Voice of the Northern Lights, to appeal for volunteers to join the police posse going after the trapper. Inspector Eames selected a force of nine men and forty-two dogs and on January 9, 1932, they arrived at the trapper's cabin.

Middleton's good friend Millen was in the posse,

and he stayed the night at the Hudson's Bay post en route to the Rat River. The two friends chatted about the hunt that lay ahead and Millen remarked: "I knew Johnson was an ugly customer, but he must be mad to shoot a policeman in cold blood." So started the name the Mad Trapper. Next day, just as Millen was leaving, he turned to Middleton and said jokingly: "Goodbye, Bob, I may not see you again." He was tragically correct. According to Middleton, Millen was shot through the forehead and killed when he deliberately raised himself up to see if the trapper would fire; other accounts state that Millen was shot through the heart in a rapid exchange of fire with the trapper. However, it is not unusual in the Mad Trapper's story for details to conflict.

The final visit by the police to the Rat River resulted in a fifteen-hour siege that ended only when the officers blew the trapper's cabin apart with a home-made dynamite bomb. But not only did the trapper survive the bombing, he escaped into the darkness and the great chase was on.

"The radio station at Aklavik broadcast the latest news of the chase every night at eight p.m. and, of course, everyone listened to it," said Middleton.

For fifty-four days, Johnson led the police on a deep winter cross-country chase in the N.W.T. and the Yukon. He engaged in four shoot-outs with the Mounties, killing one man and wounding two others. Using more than nine dog teams and, for the first time, an airplane and a portable two-way radio, the Mounties pursued and finally cornered the trapper on the Eagle River in the Yukon some 150 miles from where the chase began. During this time Johnson traveled on snowshoes which weighed ten pounds each, carted a heavy pack, and snared rabbits and squirrels for food while on the run. He seldom fired his shotgun or his two rifles for fear his pursuers would hear the shots. He died fighting on February 17, 1932. On his body was found nearly $2,500 in cash, but not a single clue to his identity.

Middleton stayed several years at Fort McPherson, made a trip home to England, and was then posted to Fort

Chipewyan, Alberta, on the shore of Lake Athabasca. From Alberta it was back to the N.W.T. again and the post at Fort Rae on Great Slave Lake. But by the time he reached Fort Rae in the 1940s, Middleton was no longer a bachelor. After a swift courtship in Winnipeg, he had married a pretty, vivacious girl named Nancy Smellie. Her father, Captain Smellie, commanded the Hudson's Bay Company's Arctic supply ship *Nascopie*, a 300-foot icebreaker, from 1917 until he retired in 1945. The *Nascopie* could carry fifty passengers, and they were usually post managers, nurses, missionaries, policemen, whalers, soldiers, explorers, and botanists.

According to a book written about Captain Smellie, *Arctic Command* by Roland Wild, all the passengers "rubbed shoulders in the crowded quarters, suffered when the ship's hot pipes froze, and slept on the floor, as the captain did, to avoid being thrown out of bed when the *Nascopie* stood on end."

"No matter how good an icebreaker you have, there are conditions in which ice will form on top of a ship," Mrs. Middleton said. "My father told me that ice can completely change the weight balance of a ship and she'll turn topsy-turvy when the ice on top gets too heavy."

The annual arrival of the ship, with its strange cargo of everything from pigs to coal, was a great event at every community. As well as vital supplies, the *Nascopie* brought the people of each place their only mail for the year. Until Captain Smellie retired, ships were the only means of supplying Arctic posts. The failure of the *Nascopie* to get through meant privation and hardship to both Eskimos and white men.

There was little Smellie did not know about ice conditions. Three times he was unable to reach Fort Ross, 960 miles from the north pole and the most northerly Hudson's Bay post, because the ice defeated him. On those occasions the company had to air lift supplies into the post, and in the early days of Arctic flying that was a hazardous job.

Bob Middleton
107

In 1947, two years after Captain Smellie retired, the *Nascopie* struck an uncharted reef and sank at Cape Dorset on Baffin Island, at the edge of Hudson's Bay.

As Mrs. Middleton talked proudly about her father's career, her only regrets were that she never made the Arctic trip with him and that he was away from his family for such long periods.

"He was away about six months every year," she said. "In fact, when my parents celebrated their fiftieth wedding anniversary, they said it was really a big joke because, in fact, they'd only lived together for twenty-five years."

Middleton had first met Nancy Smellie in Fort Smith. "Bob was doing quite a bit of work at Fort Smith for my father and I was just a schoolgirl, of course. I'd just finished grade eight," said Mrs. Middleton, who is fourteen years younger than her husband. Though still at school, Nancy was fully grown and looked much older than her age. She must have been a delightful surprise to the post manager who saw so few girls of his own British background. And he, too, made quite an impression on the teenage girl, because although she did not see him again for five years, she always sent him a card at Christmastime.

The couple met again in Winnipeg where the Smellies had moved when the *Nascopie* was placed under the management of the company's fur trade department in that city. Captain Smellie ran into Middleton in a company building and invited him home to dinner.

"We were married in six weeks," said Mrs. Middleton.

The bride's training for life in a northern outpost consisted of a bachelor of arts degree from the University of Manitoba and a brief secretarial course. "Not very helpful, really," laughed Mrs. Middleton. "But the secretarial training is coming in useful now. I had wanted to take home economics, but my father said anybody could learn how to cook and sew.

"I was married very shortly after I graduated, and

we first went together to Fort Rae, which is ninety miles north of Yellowknife."

From the civilization of Winnipeg, the young wife found herself in a house without even a kitchen sink. "We just had a dish pan and a pail, and the water was in the lake," said Mrs. Middleton. "We had to carry the water up every day. The only thing Bob had got for himself there was a thirty-two volt power plant so we had electric light, but we couldn't operate any major appliances at the same time as the lights." The thirty-two-volt gas diesel power plant became standard equipment in most Hudson's Bay posts throughout the north, but Middleton bought one of the first for himself. Mrs. Middleton, who could not even use her iron at the same time as the electric light, was not much impressed by the small electric plant.

"The joke was that Bob ordered a washing machine for me. He thought we'd get an electric washing machine, and when it arrived it was a round, wooden one," she said. "You see them in museums now—with a handle you cranked back and forth, and a hand wringer.

"So the first day I went to use it I got the water all nicely heated up on the wood stove and poured it into the washtub and immediately it ran out all over the kitchen floor. You see, I didn't know you had to let water soak into the wood to expand it when it had dried out—I was a city girl. When Bob came home from the store he asked me why I was washing the kitchen floor. After that, he decided the cranking was too much hard work for me, and got an Indian girl to come in and do the laundry."

With the girl listening to her instructions, Mrs. Middleton sorted the washing into separate piles according to color, the last being a heap of red homespun curtains.

"I told her to put the white pile in the machine first, then the next pile, and finally the red curtains," she said. "I went away to do something else and when I came back everything was in the washing machine together. The girl told me she'd put the piles in the machine in the order I told her—but she'd put them all in on top of each other. So all that winter Bob wore pink underwear, and the next time the girl came she brought a scrub board with her. She agreed with me the hand cranking was really hard work and she preferred the scrub board. So that solved my laundry problems for a while."

The next technological advance in northern washing machines was a gasoline model that had to be cranked, like an automobile, to get it going.

A washing machine of any sort would have been an undreamed-of luxury for Middleton when he first started his career with the Hudson's Bay Company, because in the early days the post manager's house, which was separate from the store, consisted of four bare walls, a kitchen table, a stove and a bed.

"Beyond that, you had to buy your own furniture," he said. "By the time I left Fort McPherson I'd completely furnished the house with things like a chesterfield suite, a rug, a radio and a few other knickknacks, and the company bought it all from me when I left. That was just at the time when they started supplying furniture in the houses, but that meant you couldn't choose your own things—the company did all the choosing."

Mrs. Middleton said accommodation gradually improved over the years, but the rules and regulations laid down by the company—such as all-white floors and ceilings—were very annoying.

"In wintertime we looked at nothing but snow outside all day long, and the last color you wanted to look at inside was white as well," said Mrs. Middleton. The company had so many complaints about the all-white rule that eventually they abandoned it and let the post managers pick their own paint colors.

There was nothing routine about the life of a post manager; in fact, it would have been a miserable existence for a man who enjoyed regular hours. A post manager had to be adaptable—or quit.

"During the depression when staff was cut way back, the workload was tremendous, especially in the spring when the furs were coming in," said Middleton. "At Fort McPherson when we were operating with two men, I once worked five days and nights without proper sleep. You worked when you had to, that was about it. And when there was no work, you took off to go duck shooting or something like that.

"You worked all kinds of different hours and the time of day made no difference at all. But I had to put my foot down as far as the store hours were concerned or else people would be bothering you all day and night."

Fort Rae was so isolated that the mail came only once a month and then the Middletons sat up all night reading letters and catching up with news.

When the trappers came in from the Barrenlands with their furs, the Middletons slaved from 7 a.m. to midnight. The rush would start at about the end of November when the men came in with just enough fur to buy supplies. They would go back to their camps, returning with their families at Christmas. Then the post store would be packed with nearly five hundred people at a time, all wearing caribou skin parkas. According to the Middletons, it felt like a steam bath at a cattle auction. After Christmas the trappers and their families vanished into the wilderness again and did not reappear until Easter.

"At Christmas we entertained everybody—it was the company custom," said Mrs. Middleton. "We had about two hundred people to the house at a time and it was a constant procession. Bob and the clerk would meet them at the door and Bob would give each man a cigar and the women some cigarettes. Then I'd have some candy for the little children. Of course, the company paid for all this."

After the candy and cigarettes procession was over, the Middletons had Christmas dinner with the opposition trader. And at New Years, the opposition trader dined with the Middletons. "At that time of the year it was peace on earth and goodwill between traders," said Mrs. Middleton. "But for the rest of the year competition was pretty keen."

An interpreter was essential for most post managers because it was impossible to cope with all the different Indian languages.

"I picked up quite a bit of Cree the first two years I was in the country, and then I moved to Fort St. John where they spoke Beaver and I decided I wasn't going to try and learn that as well," said Middleton. "From there I moved down the Mackenzie River and at Fort Smith, I think it was, they spoke Chipewyan. I was there for one year and then moved to Fort Providence where they spoke Slavey."

At Fort McPherson there was yet another language, but by then Middleton had given up all attempts to master new tongues. There was a slight relationship between some of the languages, although not enough to be very helpful.

Even the uphill work of trying to learn how to communicate with the Indians had some funny moments, as Middleton discovered when he was struggling with Cree. There was one phrase he heard repeatedly when dealing with the Indians at the store, so he memorized it and started asking people what it meant.

"I asked the store interpreter and all he said was, 'I don't know,' " said Middleton. "So then I asked the post manager and he said, 'I don't know.' I couldn't figure this out at all because the phrase was obviously a common expression; I heard it used every day."

Eventually Middleton asked his housekeeper, who was giving him lessons in Cree, and she explained that the mystery expression meant exactly what Middleton had been told all along. It meant: "I don't know."

The Middletons spent only one winter at Fort Rae and then moved southeast to Saskatchewan.

"Moving you around like that was typical—usually they moved you every three years, and the reason the company gave was that they didn't want you to get too familiar with the customers," said Mrs. Middleton. "I used to think it was foolish in a way, because you'd just get to know people and their different problems and you were moved. Then a stranger had to come in and start all over again. It was a lot of work."

The couple stayed five years at a few posts. One such was Buffalo Narrows in northern Saskatchewan, which in those days had no highway connection with the southern half of the province. The few white people who lived there were trappers and they were only around in summer; in winter they were out on their trap lines.

Middleton said he first began to notice the Indians developing a drinking problem in the early 1940s in northern Saskatchewan.

"It was white bootleggers selling hard liquor who started it," said Mrs. Middleton. "The RCMP sent a special policeman in to hunt bootleggers when we were at Buffalo Narrows. Before the bootlegging started, the natives drank all right, but it was just home brew—they'd cook up a bunch of raisins and potatoes and throw some yeast in it. But they wouldn't prepare too much of it at a time and they couldn't wait for it to get too powerful before they had a drink."

In the mid-1940s the Middletons' first child, a son, was born and three years later he was followed by another son. Mrs. Middleton went home to her mother when the babies were due, first to Winnipeg and then to Vancouver, where her parents had moved.

"The company was good in that respect—they'd foot the bill for transportation out of the post in the case of medical need," said Middleton. "Then, of course, we had radio; you could always get advice by radio."

Middleton often had to act as a doctor. In Stanley, Saskatchewan, he worked in the store during the day and bathed wounds at night. The Indians often needed medical attention because of their frequent fighting. Every post had to be well stocked with first aid equipment. Even when medical staff was available, the post manager and his wife found themselves getting involved. Once, just before freeze-up, a nurse and a pilot were stranded with them for several days because the plane's oil froze. "I thought for a while they were going to be with us for six weeks," said Mrs. Middleton. "And I had two small children and was cooking by melting ice blocks on the stove."

This chore of melting ice to get hot water was one of the more unpleasant aspects of life in the wilderness, but the post manager's wife could usually count on the interpreter to help her with the hardest jobs. However, for Mrs. Middleton who knew only the Cree words for "come" and "go away," conversation with the interpreter was strictly limited.

Educating the children in the far north was not easy. The Middletons tried various ways of arranging schooling. At first they sent the elder boy to a local school, but the teachers spent most of their time teaching the Indian children to speak English. When his parents sent him out to school in B.C., he had to repeat grade two because he was so far behind. The younger boy was educated entirely in B.C. and had no catching up to do.

In B.C. the boys went to school by bus when there was one, boarded in a Prince George dormitory, or did correspondence lessons under their mother's supervision. "I really brushed up on my grade eight arithmetic—as a matter of fact there's one problem we haven't solved yet," laughed Mrs. Middleton.

From Saskatchewan, the couple moved to Fort Simpson, B.C., but this post was on its way downhill when the Middletons arrived there. "We were sent more or less to close it down and we were only there for two winters," said Middleton.

In 1954 the couple was posted to the McLeod Lake store, on the shores of a pretty lake surrounded by birch trees. The community, named after the lake, dated back to 1806 when it was the first fur trading post built west of the Rockies by the North West Company. When the Middletons arrived, the John Hart Highway to Prince George, ninety miles south, was only two years old and was still a mess of mud holes, rock, and gravel. The drive to Prince George took three hours because there had to be constant stops to push boulders out of the way. Paving the highway was so slow that it was not finished until 1962. Before the highway was built, the only transportation link to the outside was by river boat.

The Hudson's Bay Company, which took over the North West Company, maintained the post at McLeod Lake because of the Sekani Indian reserve. By 1972 only about 130 Indians lived on the reserve, which was connected to the outside world by boat in summer or ice in winter. However, thanks to a long battle waged by Mrs. Middleton, authorities finally agreed to put a bridge across the Pack River to give the Indians a land connection with the highway. Mrs. Middleton battled for a proper bridge to replace an old log structure, because, since she had moved to McLeod Lake, at least seven Indians had drowned while making the journey from the reserve to the highway.

Mrs. Middleton gained her intimate knowledge of Indian problems first hand—for fifteen years she was drug dispenser for the department of Indian health services at McLeod Lake. In that time she coped with twenty fatalities and innumerable emergencies, all for $20 a month. She did it with the help of only a St. John's Ambulance first aid course and a home nursing course taken years previously.

"When I took on the job they said it would just be a matter of handing out a few pills and aspirins, but really it meant being virtually a doctor for the community," said Mrs. Middleton. "The Indians asked for all kinds of advice all the time and, not being a qualified nurse, I often did things that a nurse would not even have attempted to do. And Bob helped out a lot too."

The very first case she tackled involved a girl who hobbled in with a big gash across her knee. First aid was not even part of Mrs. Middleton's contract as a dispenser, but there was no one else to cope so she did her best, as she did for many more years. She cleaned up the wound, bandaged the knee and then asked the girl if she felt faint. "Oh, no, I'm fine," said the girl and walked happily away. Mrs. Middleton was the one who collapsed. "It was my first experience of a lot of blood," she explained. "But you gradually get accustomed to it."

The Middletons took the big step into business on their own in 1958 when the Hudson's Bay Company decided to close down the McLeod Lake store because of declining fur sales.

"It was a good enough business for an individual, but for a fur company with all the overhead expenses it wasn't a paying proposition," said Middleton. "So we bought the store from the Hudson's Bay; we'd moved so much that we decided to stay. 'We like it here and decided we could do a lot worse."

As owners of their own business for the first time, the Middletons dashed around in a whirlwind of activity, making the changes in the house and store they had not been able to do before. They painted, renovated, built steps and put on a new roof. When they finally got hooked up to B.C. Hydro (after years on a 110-volt diesel), acquired proper telephone service, and could drive on a blacktopped highway, they felt they were living in southern comfort, even though the winter snow at McLeod Lake is ten feet deep.

Both the Middletons have long been involved in public service, and with their sons grown up and living away from home they had more time to give to it. As well as her work as a drug dispenser, Mrs. Middleton was a director of the Fraser-Fort George Regional District board and her husband is a provincial judge for the company town of Mackenzie, about thirty miles from McLeod Lake.

The Middletons were astonished by the way Mackenzie grew up in two years from bush to a modern town complete with hospital, hotel and pulp mill.

It was a striking contrast to the tiny northern communities they were used to, which changed little over many years. Running water and electric light are something the Middletons can never learn to take for granted. As for the climate of Prince George, they find it almost tropical in comparison with the Arctic.

"I'm always surprised when people ask us how we like living here in the north," laughed Mrs. Middleton. "To us, McLeod Lake is the south."

Chapter 7
Henry Hope
Blacksmith

Henry Hope's life is a study in contradictions. Not that
Hope—he prefers to be called Harry—is a complex man.
He has the gaiety and frankness of a child, combined with a
sense of humor that bubbles through all his conversation.
Yet Hope has been deaf since the age of twelve, as a result of
measles and scarlet fever. He wanted to be a lawyer, but
ended up a blacksmith. He loves people and the stimulus of
good conversation, but has been condemned to live in a
world of silence. His frustrations have been enormous, and
yet Hope can look back on most of his life with both contentment and laughter. How did it happen?

Hope, whose father was also a blacksmith, was born

in 1883, in the north of England near Carlisle in the county of Cumberland. There were nine children in the family, six boys and three girls, and not much money to go around. "I was the youngest for seven years and then two more appeared on the scene—they were afterthoughts," said Hope, who always likes to end a sentence with a joke. "I went to a Church of England school and we had a month's holiday and worked in the fields. I worked on a farm and milked four cows a night for a penny a week."

With his intelligence and quick wit, Hope would have made an excellent lawyer—his first choice—or an auctioneer, like his grandfather and uncle. But his deafness ruled these out. The future for a deaf youth was far more restricted at the turn of the century than it is today, so Hope joined his father in the blacksmith shop when he reached the age of sixteen.

"But if it hadn't been for my deafness, I most assuredly would not have been in the blacksmith business," he said. Boys who were apprenticed blacksmiths, when Hope was young, earned about two shillings a week (the equivalent of about fifty cents today). Some only received their board and lodging, but were given a week off to earn money working in the harvest fields.

"Of course, I didn't get any money when I was living at home with my family," he said. "But I got my clothes, and if I wanted to go to a dance, I would get a shilling. You could go to a dance for a shilling then, and have a real good time. You danced from eight p.m. right through the night to four a.m. Then, if you had to walk a girl home, that'd be some distance away. So you'd just have time to get changed and go back to work. In those days, you worked from seven a.m. to seven p.m. or even nine p.m. for six days a week. In the old shop at home, we had the forge going all the time, and we had a great big pair of bellows about ten feet long. And nearly everything in the shop was hand power."

Hope soon realized that competition in the blacksmith business was getting too tough in England. His thoughts turned inevitably to Canada because his eldest brother, John, was already there. "John came home for Christmas in 1905, and told me all about it," said Hope. "In the Yukon, he'd been over the White Pass route taken by the sourdoughs, and he never got his mail for six months at a time." But these tales of the rugged north spurred Hope's interest in Canada rather than dampening it, and he was terribly excited when brother John promised to pay his fare across the Atlantic.

"He sent me a hundred and fifty dollars and that was big money in those days," said Hope. "So I bought a ticket and came to Canada in June 1906." He was twenty-two years old, deaf, and had never left home before. His ship docked in Montreal, where he immediately boarded a train for Saskatchewan. Hope's destination was Moose Jaw, because another brother was already there, working in a machine shop.

"In the caboose of the train there was a stove where you could make your own meals, but when the train stopped at divisional points for an hour or so, you could jump off and eat at cafes—that's what I did," said Hope. "In the colony cars there were no cushions, but you could lie down on the seats. Of course, you could get sleepers, but I didn't spend money on them."

Hope has been married twice. His first wife died in 1952. A few years later, he married his present wife, Mary Jane, who is three years his junior. The second Mrs. Hope was born and grew up only twelve miles from her husband's home in Cumberland, but they met for the first time in Moose Jaw. Their friendship did not end in marriage then, for Hope was on the move and Mary Jane was a teenager, still living with her parents.

In Moose Jaw, Hope inevitably found himself working in the blacksmith's shop, earning real money for the first time in his life. "We worked from seven a.m. to about six p.m. for three dollars a day, and everybody was very happy and contented," said Hope. "You could get a good square meal in a cafe for twenty-five cents, and that dinner today would cost you two dollars and fifty cents." The only problem was that he did not like Moose Jaw. "The bald, flat prairies didn't appeal to me at all," he said. "But at the Moose Jaw fair, I saw exhibits of wonderful apples and all kinds of fruit from the Okanagan in big glass jars and I thought, that's the place for me."

Hope never wasted any time once he had made up his mind. By October 1906, he had said goodbye to the prairies and travelled as far west as Golden in British Columbia. He found himself a blacksmith's job at a logging camp in the community of Athalmer, about ninety miles south of Golden near the B.C.-Alberta border, and here, Canada at last began to come up to his expectations.

"I spent four and a half months at that camp—it was one of the happiest times of my life there. Oh boy, the cooking was lovely," he said. "We used to get our breakfast about six a.m. and the gang would be out working by seven a.m. Then at about half past nine I'd go to the cookhouse for a snack. At noon I could have anything that was going—a beef steak or pork chops or something like that. Then there was afternoon tea, you know, oh rather."

The drawback to camp life that Hope never forgot was the absence of women. "In the four and a half months I was there, I only saw one woman, and she was the foreman's wife," he recalled. "The foreman brought her in from Athalmer and I had quite a chat with her."

At the logging camp, Hope was kept very busy shoeing horses, fixing sleighs, and making all kinds of logging tools, such as cant hooks, which are used for rolling logs. "We used to take a piece of cant hook steel and cut it off to a certain length, eighteen inches long, then set it to six inches back by hand, then pound it out to a hook and shape it," said Hope. "The band, clasp and everything was made by hand. It was very, very interesting."

Every evening in camp, there were long debates on every topic under the sun as the men sat around the stove.

"I was only twenty-three at the time and I told them I believed in the Golden Rule—do as you would be done by," said Hope. "A Yankee told me he admired my philosophy, but reckoned I would never get anywhere in this country until I adopted the Yankee Philosophy—do the other SOB before he does you."

The camp was only a few miles from Radium Hot Springs, now a popular resort because of its year-round hot spring pools. At the time Hope was blind to its potential, and so missed what he has always believed was a great opportunity.

"In February one of the chaps got rheumatism and said he was going to the springs for a cure," said Hope. "He came back in about two weeks and I asked him how he panned out. He jumped up and down in the cabin, clapped his hands together and said, 'Boy, oh boy, Harry, that's the cat's whiskers.'" He urged Hope to join him homesteading in the Radium Hot Springs area, but the young blacksmith was dubious. "In those days it took us two days to go with horse and team from Golden to Athalmer, because it was just a winding trail," explained Hope. "Of course, I couldn't see with a fifty-foot spyglass in those days. But now I believe we could have homesteaded the blessed thing. Today it's about a twelve million dollar proposition and a beautiful place."

Hope, of course, still had his heart set on the Okanagan and had no wish to be sidetracked to the wilderness at the foot of the Rocky Mountains. So in April 1907, he left the camp and made his way alone to Vernon where, as usual, he found himself a job as a blacksmith. At last he was working in the Okanagan that he had dreamed about for months—but he did not think much of Vernon.

"I never liked the place, because there were too many damned English people there putting on the dog, though they didn't have a bean," he said. "I was staying at the Coldstream Hotel and, after I'd finished for the day, I'd go to the hotel, get freshened up and changed, and have dinner about six p.m. One day, this bloody Englishman (excuse my language) came up to me and said, 'Hope, no one would think you were a blacksmith when you get all dressed up.' And I said to him, 'It's no sin to be a hewer of wood and a drawer of water. I can pay my bill and I don't have to go and borrow money like you so-and-so's do.' I gave him the works." And Hope chuckled at the memory of his little speech that had left the arrogant Englishman with his mouth hanging open.

During his 1907 stay in Vernon, Hope had his first look at Vancouver. "I stayed there for five days and it rained for four and a half—that was in November," he said. "I figured I might have stayed there, but not with all that rain. I said, 'Goodbye, Vancouver, I'm not a duck' and went back to the sunny Okanagan. It's probably still raining down there. All I can remember of Vancouver then was smog; you couldn't see the damn place for smoke, because everyone was burning stumps."

In October 1907, Hope's Vernon job came to an end. He went to nearby Armstrong and found a job with the local blacksmith.

A B.C. government road sign outside Armstrong marks the early days of this countryside known as the Spallumcheen Valley. The sign reads:

"And our eyes feasted on the long stretch of Prairies..." wrote A.L. Fortune, first settler in this fertile valley, in June 1866. The natural meadows, rippling in tall grasses, were ideal pasture for cattle and sheep. Later, grain replaced livestock. Despite many decades of use, 'Spil-a-mi-shine' of the Indians remains ever bountiful, ever beautiful.

The words of the sign help to explain Hope's contentment with his life. Despite the frustrating handicap of deafness, he has lived most of his days in a beautiful and fertile land that he loves.

Henry Hope
123

Armstrong, which is in the north Okanagan, was once the hunting ground of the Shuswap Indians. These Indians were probably the most fortunate in Canada, because their lakes and rivers always had salmon and kokanee runs, large herds of deer roaming the forests, and a valley that was the biggest chokeberry and saskatoon patch in B.C. The climate was pleasant and there was never a shortage of fish or game.

Armstrong was named in 1892 after W.C. Heaton-Armstrong, head of a London banking house which floated the bonds to build the Sicamous and Okanagan railway. The railway was then and still is important to Armstrong's economy, with both the Canadian Pacific and Canadian National trains running freight. The tracks run through the middle of town; the main street is appropriately named Railway Avenue. Trains shunt to and fro across this street all day long, and the residents do not even seem to notice them.

One of the biggest tourist attractions in town is Hope's blacksmith shop, still in its original wooden building, which he reckons dates back to before 1900. The shop itself is a glorious muddle of metal. Horseshoes are nailed to the low beams of the ceiling and strange-looking equipment—some of it not used for decades—clutters every corner of the building.

Hope worked in Armstrong until the spring of 1908, a year when the small community was busy expanding and organizing its great farming capacity. The land was being cleared with the aid of main force and stumping powder. First, the trees were cut down with crosscut saws and axes. Then, the stumps were blown out of the ground with several sticks of blasting powder. Finally, horses were used to remove the trees and pull out the remaining roots. The holes that were left were filled in with earth and the brush was gathered up by hand, heaped into piles, and burned. "In May 1908, we had a bee to clear stumps in Armstrong and we were all digging with teams of horses and one thing and another," said Hope. "It was a hot summer and the publicans and sinners at the hotel sent us down a keg of beer to wet our whistles. There was enough for a couple of snifters for everyone and that was okay with us. The people here were very friendly and helpful and got together all the time."

Medical aid was not available then, and Hope recalled a terrible accident which befell a friend of his named Frank Young. "He got his arm caught in a threshing machine and he had to have it amputated without anesthetic," said Hope. "So they got him drunk and held him down on a table. One of the men who held him down was his father, who drove a six-horse team on the Cariboo Highway. A man who was a vet cut off Frank's arm with a butcher knife and then put the stub in a bag of flour to stop the bleeding. He recovered.

"The blacksmith wanted me to buy his business in Armstrong, but I wasn't ready to settle. Instead I went back to Vernon and went farming and had a jolly good time."

After two years of bachelor fun, Hope decided to buckle down to the business of earning a living, because there was a girl back in England whom he could not get out of his mind. "So I came back here to Armstrong and bought the blacksmith's business in November 1910, and I've been here ever since," said Hope. That year, Armstrong appointed its first fire chief at a salary of $15 a year, and the building inspector earned $60 a year. There was plenty of work in the growing town, and Hope was kept busy shoeing horses, fixing sleighs, making ploughshares, shaping cattle brands, and repairing farm equipment.

"In 1910, we were charging five dollars for eight new cork horse shoes, and mind you, that included the nails and everything, by gosh," said Hope. "Sometimes you'd spend two to three hours on a bronc and get nothing extra. I'd have to check my records, but I'll bet you that during the Depression we were still getting no more than eight dollars for eight new shoes.

Henry Hope
125

"I boarded in the Armstrong Hotel in the early days—it's the same one that's standing today," he said. "I had the best room in the house and wonderful food, all you could eat, and it cost thirty-five dollars a month. In those days, there were a lot of farms dotted around, homesteaders you know, but not many people living in town. The farmers had a tough time clearing off the land and there were an awful lot of stumps around for years, but finally they all got blown out and the street widened. All the logs went to the mill in winter. I think they got four dollars or four dollars and fifty cents a thousand board foot at the mill. So that helped pay for the groceries and one thing and another.

"I remember the winter of 1910 was particularly cold and the town had hired an ex-Mountie to make foot patrols in the evening," said Hope. "One night there was a bit of a prayer meeting, a revival meeting, going on at the old Methodist church, and the Mountie dropped in there to get warmed up. He sat down at the back and thought no one would notice. Well, there was a very old patriarch Methodist at the meeting—we used to call him Sir John Moore—and he went and tapped the Mountie on the shoulder and asked, 'Have you found Jesus yet?' The Mountie replied, 'I've never been advised he was lost.' " And Hope doubled up with laughter at his story.

"In the winter time it was lovely here, with the sleighs and the sleigh bells and the people coming in for church services," he said. "Those were happy days, you bet. There were a lot of church socials then, and we bachelors used to play the field." Hope was still thinking about his girl back in England, so he decided to take a trip home.

Since coming to Canada, he had corresponded with a girl named Emily, who lived only two miles from his old home. "She was my childhood sweetheart, you might say, because I'd known her since she was a little girl," he said. "She was a lovely girl, very, very fair. And she was also very shy. I was often at her home in England and she wrote to me once in a while, after I came to Canada. Once, when I hadn't heard from her for a while, she sent me a card that said, 'If a body writes a body, getting no reply, may a body ask a body, what's the reason why?' " Whatever hopes Emily had of a romantic reply were soon dashed. Hope sent her back a card carrying just the one word, "No," but as usual, he was only joking.

When he made his trip to England in 1912, he visited Emily at her home. They became engaged almost immediately, but it was to be a long engagement. "Her father said he was happy and would we like to get married right away," said Hope. "But I said no, because I wanted to get a nice home for her and get it furnished. She had been educated in a private school and she was very fond of glass and paintings."

While he was in England, Hope made one last attempt to find a cure for his deafness. "I went to three ear, nose, and throat hospitals in London and then I saw Dr. Hunter Todd, a Harley Street consultant who was a two-guinea-a-shot man," said Hope. "I said I'd give five hundred dollars in dollar bills if he could cure my deafness. But he laid his cards on the table. He said there was no cure for my kind of deafness and he told me to forget about it."

Hope then realized that he would have to live with his deafness forever. He could lip read fairly well and seemed to have a second sense of what people were saying to him. But this was no substitute for real hearing, and Hope was painfully aware of all that he was missing. Many men would have sunk into depression. Not Hope. He fumed at his fate—and then resumed his good humor. And in 1912, not even deafness could dim the joy of having his own girl.

Hope's plan was to return to Canada, sell some real estate he owned in Moose Jaw, build a home for Emily, and go back for her in two years' time. "I thought I'd make two thousand dollars on the real estate, but the bottom fell out of the market," said Hope. So instead of going back to

England to claim his bride, he asked some friends of his who were visiting there to bring her to Canada with them. "She came out to me and we were married here in Armstrong in March 1914."

The English bride found herself in a beautiful but isolated farming community. The stump-filled bush of the turn of the century had vanished, but western Canada was still the edge of the world for someone from Europe. The records of the municipal council give some revealing glimpses of early life in Armstrong. In 1911, for instance, moving pictures came to town and in the same year the municipal clerk started using a typewriter to record the minutes. In 1912, men working for the municipality were paid $2.50 a day for a ten-hour day—except for Saturdays, when it was nine hours.

The farms scattered around Armstrong were doing so well that bumper crops of potatoes, celery, lettuce and other vegetables were shipped out of the valley every year. Swamp lands near town were drained and turned into productive meadows. "In the early days, all that bottom land was under cultivation by the Chinese, and it was a beautiful picture," said Hope. "There must have been about two hundred Chinese in here in the early days—I don't know the exact number. But I'll tell you what happened to the Chinese: the packing houses took them to the cleaners." Hope meant that the Chinese laborers were paid the absolute minimum the six packing houses, owned by white men, could get away with.

Chinese workers were first hired in Armstrong to work in the celery fields, which began production in 1904 and were phenomenally successful. The first crop yielded 300 pounds and by 1910, the harvest had soared to 400 tons. In Armstrong, two crops of celery and two of lettuce can be grown every year. But in those days, a lot of back-breaking labor went into the production of a good celery crop.

The Chinese received between $15 and $160 a ton

for the celery. The price varied each year, but averaged $60 a ton. On top of this hard work and low pay, many of the Chinese workers lived in overcrowded boarding houses, which, even in 1911, were considered a health hazard. But they stayed on, and some of them learned the job so well that they put the white growers out of business. None of them became rich, however, because they were always up against the white-owned packing houses.

Hope was constantly annoyed by the exploitation of the Chinese, whom he considered his best customers. "I liked them because they would always mind their own business, they paid their bills, and if you did them a favor they would never forget it," he said. But Hope was way ahead of his time in his thinking. Prejudice against the Chinese was far more common than tolerance.

The war 6,000 miles away in Europe at first had little effect on Armstrong. But by the time the Armistice was signed, Armstrong had lost fifty-five men. For Hope, the end of the war meant that he could start building the house he had long planned for his wife.

"I built the house with the help of two professional old country carpenters, who worked for a dollar an hour," he said. "Those were the days when the best Scotch was a dollar for a twenty-six-ounce bottle." Hope bought the two lots on which the house is built for a total of $750. "Shiplap in those days was sixteen dollars a thousand; now it's close to two hundred dollars," he said. "A local factory made all the doors, window frames and woodwork. Between you and me and the gatepost, I think all the fittings, including the windows, came to about four hundred and eighty dollars. And that was workmanship in those days. Houses were built to last."

The Roaring Twenties passed by the Hopes and Armstrong, because both the family and the community were working too hard to be frivolous. The Armstrong *Advertiser* reported that cars were getting "so thick on the streets that it's almost as dangerous to drive as it is to walk.

The chauffeur needs to be careful, now, not only because he is liable to run over somebody, but because he is liable to get mangled in a wreck." Ford cars sold for $741.35, but at least someone else in town besides Hope had a sense of humor, because the following advertisement was placed in the *Advertiser* in 1922:

> I have some hens I do not want
> Let whoever wants them holler;
> They are young and fat and laying eggs.
> For each I want a dollar.
> The price you know is not absurd,
> But very fair—see Mrs. Bird.

In 1923, sirloin steak sold for sixteen cents a pound and good farm land for $15 an acre. In 1924 came the plebiscite to decide whether to have the retail sale of beer introduced—Armstrong voted no.

1924 was also the year when radios were sold in Armstrong for the first time and a man was fined $10 for driving over fifteen miles an hour on the main street. Thirteen people were charged with offenses during the year— one for the crime of "seduction under promise of marriage."

The Depression had its effect on the Okanagan, too, and Hope remembers it as a grim period for many people. "We lost a lot of men who went away, and there were many bad debts when people lost money," he said. In February 1932, about seventy unemployed men marched into Armstrong from Vernon, where they had been living in a relief camp for several months. They were en route to Victoria to lay their griefs before the provincial government. The invasion stirred both sympathy and fear in the people of Armstrong and they offered the men shelter and a meal. The unemployed bedded down for the night and next day, they left peaceably.

A good deal of Hope's fun in life, which enabled him to put up with his deafness, resulted from his long association with the Armstrong *Advertiser* and with the Jamieson family who owned it. The newspaper was established in 1902 and had a string of different owners before it was sold in 1927 to John E. Jamieson. Jamieson, who died in 1954, handed on the business to his sons, James (Jim) and John. The third generation Jamieson to get involved in running the paper was John's son, Jack.

Every morning for more than fifty years, Hope has gone into the newspaper office and, if he has a news item, he earns his daily pay—a penny. "My dad did that before me, and it's carried on ever since," said John Jamieson. "Mr. Hope calls himself our shop foreman and he's still strong as a horse. He must be the only practicing blacksmith in B.C.—the others have all become welders. He still turns out a lot of ploughshares for the farmers here—he's very adaptable. Everyone in Armstrong loves him and he makes himself known to everyone. He has the news before anyone else. He's the most wonderful man I have ever met."

"On account of my deafness I couldn't take much part in civic matters," said Hope wistfully. Informally, he was very active about Armstrong's long-standing water shortage problems—arguing his case with anyone who would listen. And he was successful. Partly as a result of his suggestions, the dam on Silver Star Lake was built and the available water supply was almost doubled.

In 1955, about three years after the death of his first wife, Hope married again. His second wife, whom he had first met nearly fifty years previously in Moose Jaw, had been a widow for more than ten years when he talked her into matrimony for the second time. "I never intended marrying again, but I was alone and he was alone, so it seemed like a good idea," said Mrs. Hope.

"One Christmas, I was sending a card to Mr. Hope's brother and sister-in-law, who were friends of mine in Vancouver, and I thought I'd send Harry a card too," said Mrs. Hope. "Well, by golly, after that the letters went back and forth and we got married."

Henry Hope
131

"Think young and you keep young. My motto is think happy and be happy," laughed Hope. "If I'd had my hearing, nobody could have lived with me." His wife was much nearer the truth when she said, "He could have been such a man, if it hadn't been for his deafness."

Hope shoed his last horse in 1971, because there was no longer enough money in it. "People want their horses shod for nothing, that's the trouble," he explained. "Until a few years ago I was charging twelve dollars for four hand-forged shoes—and that included trimming the horse's feet and putting the shoes on. But now these people with saddle horses are status seekers with damn little money, and they said twelve dollars was too much. So I told them to get lost."

As he moved into his eighties, Hope used his shop as a hobby and opened up for business only when he felt like it. But he did a little work nearly every day—making cattle brands or doing some acetylene welding, because he was convinced the activity kept him fit. He drove from home to his shop in his ancient car, clashing gears as he went, quite unable to hear the din.

In recent years, tourists often outnumber customers in Hope's shop. He likes to talk to them, but gets annoyed when they ask for souvenirs of the old days, like wagon wheels. He has all kinds of antiques, such as sleighs and farm machinery, tucked away on the top floor of his shop, but tourists are never invited that far.

Hope's party piece is to play his "orchestra": the machinery in his shop. He gets it all going at the same time, making different noises—the triphammer he calls the bongo drums—and takes a childlike delight in watching the astonished faces of visiting tourists. Of course, he can hear nothing of the "music" he makes.

"A man from Oregon was in here the other day, and I told him to make himself welcome and look around," said Hope. "Then he pulled out a bunch of tracts and asked me if I was saved. I was equal to the occasion. I said I was the only Hope for mankind." Hope, as usual, had the last word.

Chapter 8
Alan Innes-Taylor
Mountie, Riverboat Man

Alan Innes-Taylor has been a policeman, a riverboat purser, a dog handler for an Antarctic expedition, an inventor, a specialist in cold weather survival techniques, an airline consultant, and a motion picture technical adviser. And that is probably not a full list, because Innes-Taylor hates to talk about himself.

Everything about Innes-Taylor comes as a surprise. He was born in England in 1901 and brought to Canada at the age of five by his parents, who themselves had fascinating backgrounds. They were originally New Zealanders, and his father had run sugar plantations in Central America before moving to Canada and settling in rural Ontario in

1906. His mother was a professional singer who had taught music and singing at a conservatory in Toronto.

The First World War broke up the family. Innes-Taylor's father volunteered for the army and was killed. His mother went to Belgium and did relief work among refugee children, was wounded, and decorated for her work by the King of Belgium. She never returned to Canada, and died in German-occupied Belgium during the Second World War.

Young Innes-Taylor was only a teenager during the 1914-18 war, but shortly before the war ended he joined the RAF and became a pilot. "The RAF did all the training of Canadians in those days, and I was flying for the last few months of the war," he said. "I flew in Canada and Britain, but I never made it into active combat." When the war was over he headed back to Canada and the north. "I'd heard stories about the north as a boy and that's why I headed up there as soon as I got a chance."

Before he was twenty, Innes-Taylor joined the Royal Northwest Mounted Police which, in 1919, changed its name to the Royal Canadian Mounted Police. The entry qualifications were rugged. A man had to be over six feet tall, willing to stay unmarried for twelve years, and prepared to live on $45 a month plus room and board.

"Of course, a married man could not have lived on that pay anyway, even if he was posted to the Northwest Territories or the Yukon and got an extra fifty cents a day," he said. "There were around fifteen or sixteen hundred men in the force when I joined it with my brother—there were just the two of us in the family—and we were by no means the youngest members. The RCMP took on boys of sixteen then as trumpeters and when they were eighteen they were allowed to become proper members of the force."

Innes-Taylor did his basic training in Regina and was then dispatched to Vancouver where labor unrest had followed the end of the First World War. Coping with labor demonstrations in the fledgling metropolis of Vancouver was an experience, but it was not the northern challenge that Innes-Taylor had dreamed about. What he did find interesting, however, was the short period he spent on the almost hopeless task of trying to stop opium smuggling into Canada by the Chinese. This racket was an old problem for the Lower Mainland police. During the latter half of the nineteenth century, when it was a legal business, tons of opium were manufactured each year in B.C. The drug was then smuggled into the U.S., to the fury and frustration of American customs officials. Victoria, briefly fancying itself part of the Wild West, was the headquarters of the smugglers, until the federal government ended legal traffic in narcotics in 1908.

"After that, the opium used to come into Canada from the Far East by ship, because the Chinese here wanted it for their own use," said Innes-Taylor. "The system was that when a big ship reached the Georgia Strait the opium would be put into a barrel and thrown overboard, where it would be picked up by a waiting small boat. That's how the RCMP got involved—trying to stop the smuggling into B.C. But the Chinese are about the best smugglers in the world; they are real experts, and we never did catch anyone red-handed with a barrel of opium. In fact, we didn't even make any arrests that I can recall. Most of the crews of the CPR ships like the *Empress of Canada* and the *Empress of Japan* were Chinese in those days, and they were the fellows who threw the opium overboard to a waiting fishing boat. The smuggling went on for years all along the coast, but especially in the port of Vancouver."

Soon, however, Innes-Taylor left the soft life of southern B.C. and achieved his ambition of being posted to the Yukon. In the early 1920s, the Mounties patrolled with horses and pack animals. The only road in the north was the winter Dawson City-Whitehorse route, along which the White Pass and Yukon Route company used about three hundred head of horses.

"In those days all the people in the territory lived

along the Yukon River between Whitehorse and Dawson," said Innes-Taylor. "It was a very law-abiding part of the world then, because it had to be. If you committed a crime, where would you go? There were no roads to escape on. You either had to go up the river or down the river, so it was a pretty poor place for criminals. The result was that we Mounties acted in the same way as the early police in the 1870s when the prairies were being settled by homesteaders. The police were there to protect them and help them, and the same thing was true in the Yukon when I was in the RCMP. If a man was building a cabin, you'd stop and give him a hand for a few days."

Five years in the RCMP was long enough for Innes-Taylor because, as he explained it with his usual simplicity, "I had other things I wanted to do." He joined the White Pass and Yukon Route company as a riverboat purser and soon knew every bend and current in the Yukon River, the artery of the territory. At that time, the White Pass and Yukon Route provided the only transportation linking the territory to the outside world, and the history of the company goes hand in hand with the history of the Yukon.

Sparked by the Klondike gold rush in 1898, the White Pass and Yukon Route railway was built to connect the Yukon to the sea at Skagway, Alaska, and the trains are still running today. The building of this 110-mile railroad through the mountains and over the Chilkoot Pass has been described as the toughest railway construction job ever undertaken. With nothing but horses, black-powder and men, the work crews blasted and hacked their way through the granite until the golden spike was hammered home in July 1900. Within months of the railway's completion, the company inaugurated its river division.

Using coastal steamers as well as White Pass rail and riverboat services, it was possible by 1901 to travel first class from Seattle to Dawson City in only eight days. The river division developed rapidly into a fleet of some 250 sternwheel steamers and barges that plied the Yukon River and its tributaries for more than fifty years. Innes-Taylor signed on with the White Pass riverboat *Casca* as a purser when he left the Mounties and soon found it was nothing like the glamorous life of a purser on an Atlantic liner.

"A purser on the riverboats had to do everything," he said. "We handled all the freight invoices and we measured the wood that was brought aboard from the woodcutters living along the river. We even had to do the woodcutters' shopping for them, because they lived very lonely lives. They were always glad to see you, those woodcutters, and they'd hang a white shirt out near their cabin as a signal when they wanted the boat to stop. So we'd stop and see what they wanted and take their shopping orders from them.

"They were a tough race of men and most of them never married; they died bachelors, which is a pity because none of their strong progeny was left behind in the world. They were men who rather enjoyed their lonely lives, because I often noticed they got uncomfortable if you stayed too long with them. I sometimes used to visit them in the winter and stayed overnight, sitting up all night talking because were so eager to know what was going on in the world. But next day you could tell, if you knew them well, that they'd just as soon you moved on. That didn't mean they were unfriendly, it was just the way they were."

The woodcutters cut wood all winter and hauled it with the aid of their horses to the river bank where it was easy to load onto the steamers. It took between 8,000 and 10,000 cords of wood to supply all the boats during the season. "The boats I went on did the four hundred and sixty-mile trip between Whitehorse and Dawson," recalled Innes-Taylor. "In those days it took thirty-six hours to make the trip to Dawson, but it took four and a half days to come back up. It was fighting the currents of never less than five miles per hour that took so long on the return trip. Occasionally, boats would get hung up on a sandbar for a few hours, and sometimes there was a gale blowing on Lake

LeBarge which buffeted the shallow-draft vessels so much that their steam pipes were in danger of splitting."

The riverboats were not merely freight carriers. As early as 1924, most of the boat passengers were tourists, and the big Whitehorse-to-Dawson vessels carried as many as 100 first-class passengers as well as 300 tons of cargo. On the largest boat, the 406-ton *Klondike*, there were dances every night after the dining room waiters cleared away the china, the ornate flatware, and the heavy silver coffee pots.

There were no bars or radios aboard the ships. The tourists brought their own bottles and entertained themselves by sitting on deck, watching the scenery, and going ashore at the wood camps and trading posts. "In an emergency we could land along the river bank almost anywhere and, taking our battery telephone hook-up, run the long wire over the telegraph line and talk to the nearest telegraph station, usually about twenty or thirty miles away," said Innes-Taylor. "The station operator would relay the message either up to Whitehorse or down to Dawson."

In winter, the boats were pulled up on the river bank and completely overhauled. Hulls were repaired, canvas-covered decks patched and painted, and boilers cleaned. Every vessel was painted inside and out. The ships had to be ready by May 15, so that they could be launched as soon as the ice went out. "Launching was a sideways job with two men simultaneously cutting the forward and aft lines and letting the ship slide down the greasy ways into the river," said Innes-Taylor.

The first trip down the river every year was the one that he and all the riverboat crews remembered best. "It was always exciting because each year there were changing sandbars, shifting channels to contend with," said Innes-Taylor.

Some years the ice in Lake LeBarge went out in May, but more often it was June—usually the 10th but sometimes as late as the 15th. "It was always a chancy business for the first ship into the lake, until the company started spreading a mixture of old crank case oil and lamp black over an area wide enough to take a ship from one end of the lake to the other," said Innes-Taylor. "This mixture quickly rotted out a channel and then the first ship was loaded. Passengers were boarded, and most of them on that first trip were miners returning to Dawson and drummers—which was the name in those days for traveling salesmen.

"Freight on the first boat consisted of fresh fruit, vegetables, and eggs—the latter to replace those old candled eggs," recalled Innes-Taylor. "The fresh eggs were brought in over ice, but carefully kept from freezing, and they cost two dollars a dozen. I remember one old-timer who complained that the fresh eggs just didn't taste right and he demanded instead some of 'those Yukon eggs with real flavor.' "

The skipper felt like the most important person in the world, standing in the wheelhouse as the first boat of the season berthed at Dawson, with all the townspeople waving and cheering. The schoolchildren were given a holiday to see the boat arrive.

The last trip of the season was as sad as the first was happy, because the boat left behind a community largely cut off from the rest of the world, save for the occasional bush pilot and the mail coaches.

"The last boat out of Dawson could be as late as mid-October, but generally it was September," said Innes-Taylor. The ship was jammed with passengers: woodcutters and their horses, trappers with their dog teams, and prospectors going out from their claims. "It was tough for those who watched the old-timers leaving, knowing that many of them would never return."

When the last whistle finally blew, there were many tears both ashore and on board, because things would never be quite the same again.

The last trip upstream in the fall was a long one, because the river was low and the steamer often got stuck on sandbars. Once Innes-Taylor's boat stuck fast on a sandbar and was soon desperately short of wood, but the nearest woodcutter was uncooperative because the ship's skipper had previously turned down his small stock of eleven cords.

"When the old woodcutter came on board he said the price of his wood was now twenty dollars a cord instead of ten dollars—inasmuch as we'd turned him down the first time," said Innes-Taylor. "We took all he had, but by the time we got off the bar we'd had to cut green wood, and our trip home was so slow it was early October before we finally reached Whitehorse."

Innes-Taylor particularly remembered Percy De Wolfe, who ran the mail once a month from Dawson to Eagle, Alaska, after the ships stopped running for the winter. Whether ice was running in the river or not, Percy never missed his mail run, which was eighty miles as the crow flies but probably half as much again following the winding river. "Starting out with his dog team and sled and the mail in his long canoe, he would go until he came to the end of water," said Innes-Taylor. "Then he would load his sled, hook up the dogs, and go on until he came to open water again. In all the years he never missed getting out the mail, whether it was sixty below or the spring thaw."

There was a short period when even the mail did not get through to Dawson, but stage coaches soon started operating with four-horse teams on the 345-mile run in winter and spring. The horses were changed every twenty to thirty miles at the various road houses like Takhini, Little River, Carmacks, Minto, and Summit. At a stop appropriately named Yukon Crossing, the passengers had to cross the river by canoe, or if there was ice running, wait until it was safe to walk across. And that wait could be as long as ten or fifteen days, depending on the weather.

"In those days, those of us who worked on the river knew nearly everyone in the Yukon," said Innes-Taylor. "We all knew each other—trappers, pilots, miners, traders, and prospectors—and every man's word was his bond.

There was almost no crime, and although there was the odd happy drunk, there was no alcoholism problem. When I first knew Whitehorse, it was a small village with a couple of hundred people. Horses wandered downtown and no one worried about them and there were exactly two Model T's in town. But most of Whitehorse was a farming area owned by a man named Charlie Baxter, one of the two big game guides in the territory.

"They were good sailing days along the Yukon River, but many ships were eventually wrecked or sunk. The *Philip B. Low* sank so many times, it became known as the *Fill-up Below*." In the winter; when the boats had been hauled out of the river, Innes-Taylor did not take off for a few months of sunshine as some Yukoners did. He stayed right there in the territory, where the temperatures often plunged to sixty below, and worked underground in the silver, lead and zinc mines in the Keno and Mayo area.

But Innes-Taylor did leave the Yukon occasionally and in 1928, when he was on his way back from a California vacation, he received a message that led him into one of the strangest adventures of his life. "I was passing through Vancouver, and the White Pass agent there asked me if I knew where he could get some dogs for the Antarctic explorer, Admiral Byrd," he said. With his usual aplomb, Innes-Taylor replied that, yes, as a matter of fact, he did know where he could get some dogs. "I asked how soon the dogs were wanted and the answer was they had to sail tomorrow."

Apparently, Admiral Richard Byrd, then waiting for supplies at his base at Little America in the Bay of Whales on the Antarctic coast, had recently lost a group of pack dogs. The South Pole-bound animals, accustomed to the low temperatures of the north, had died on board ship in the tropics because they had been fed the wrong diet. Now the explorer need replacements, and needed them so quickly that Innes-Taylor doubted it could be done. But he headed immediately up Grouse Mountain in North Vancouver, where he knew that a man named Pat Hardy had a ski camp and kept a pack of huskies. "Sure enough, Hardy was able to help me. I bought thirty dogs from him and sailed with them the following day," he said.

Hardy recalled the day when Innes-Taylor arrived with his strange request. "He sat down with me and I figured out a diet for the dogs, so that they wouldn't die in the heat of the equator," said Hardy, who trained dogs all over Canada at one time or another. "He has a wonderful brain, that fellow Innes-Taylor, and I figured he'd learn from the dogs, particularly the leaders. The leaders knew more than I did myself. They had fourteen calls and could remember them from year to year. I'd trained those dogs with kindness and never used a whip on them. In those days people thought the only way to train a dog was to use force, but that wasn't my way. An honest dog, if it's treated kindly, will do anything for you—he'll protect you and even starve for you."

Hardy's faith in his dogs was justified. They survived all kinds of traveling in all kinds of weather. And traveling with them all the time, much to his surprise, was Innes-Taylor.

He delivered the dogs to the port of Vancouver, as per instructions, and then planned to return to Whitehorse. But the passenger ship, the *Niagara*, suddenly went back on its agreement to carry the dogs for fear they might disturb the passengers. "We finally agreed, after considerable talk and negotiation, that I would go to New Zealand with the animals and then return to the Yukon," said Innes-Taylor. "I had no idea of going to the Antarctic at the time, but we had to get the dogs there somehow."

When the *Niagara* reached New Zealand, the dogs had to go into quarantine, so Innes-Taylor stayed to look after them. After several months' delay, he finally reached the Antarctic, but his arrival was an anticlimax. It was late 1929 and the expedition was packing up to go home. On

November 28 and 29 of that year, Byrd and his chief pilot, Bernt Balchen, had achieved their objective of flying over the South Pole.

However, Innes-Taylor's long voyage had not been made in vain. Byrd recognized him as an expert handler of dogs, and invited him to join his next expedition to the Antarctic the following year. When the expedition headed back to the Antarctic again, Innes-Taylor was the chief of field operations and had 160 dogs to look after, as well as some Citröen tractors. "This was a much bigger expedition than Admiral Byrd's previous ones and undertook some elaborate scientific research programs," he said. "The admiral was a fine man and very easy to get along with."

Even Innes-Taylor had had enough of ice and cold after his many months in the Antarctic, so when the expedition was over, he did not head back immediately to the Yukon. Instead, his wanderings took him to the dusty Texas plains, where he worked as an oil scout for a petroleum company. The job of an oil scout is to search for potentially productive drilling sites and it is hard, hot work which calls for lots of luck as well as skill. "The scouts used to meet once a week," Innes-Taylor recalled, "and we'd exchange information before going out in the field for core samples and other indicators of a good find."

Once, he ran up against the vast empire of the multi-millionaire and newspaper tycoon William Randolph Hearst. Some of Hearst's army of staff chased him off a Mexican oil development, and this sort of ruthless pursuit of the dollar did not suit the gentle Yukoner at all.

Soon Innes-Taylor was back again in the land he loved the best. "There wasn't really any Depression in the north," he said. "People there may have been poor, but they always had enough food and clothing to get by on. I think depressions can be seen and felt in crowded places, but not in the wilderness."

When the ex-pilot, ex-Mountie, ex-dog trainer, and ex-oil scout came back to the territory, he worked at a variety of jobs but was continually adding to his enormous knowledge of cold weather survival techniques. He invented all kinds of Arctic gear, such as a life raft with an inflatable canopy that could be buried under snow as a sort of portable igloo. His lightweight hollow axe could be filled with water which froze and gave the blade the necessary weight. Another invention was a four-person sleeping bag, which used the shared body warmth of the occupants to keep each person much warmer than an individual bag could.

Soon, Innes-Taylor became recognized as one of North America's experts in Arctic survival, and when the Second World War started he was snapped up by the U.S. Air Force. The English-born Canadian became a captain in the U.S. Air Force and ended the war with the rank of Lieutenant-Colonel. "It was unique for a Canadian," he admitted.

The U.S. Air Force was flying many planes from Goose Bay, Labrador, over Greenland and Iceland to Prestwick, Scotland, during the war and Innes-Taylor helped to organize the search and rescue techniques for that icy and hazardous route. He had been at it for almost a year when he was recalled to the U.S. to set up survival schools for airmen who were likely to come down over frozen territory.

"By the end of the war I had five schools organized in the U.S. and Canada with about five hundred to a thousand students a month going through them," said Innes-Taylor. "It was interesting and necessary work but not terribly exciting." Exciting it may not have been, but the Americans thought so highly of their borrowed Canadian that they awarded him the Congressional Medal of Honor.

While Innes-Taylor was away doing his war work, the peace and isolation of his northern corner of Canada was changing rapidly. In 1942 the Alaska Highway was built, connecting Dawson Creek, B.C., to Fairbanks, Alaska, and pushing a major highway through the southern Yukon.

At the height of construction, 30,000 men arrived in Whitehorse and the last frontier got another shove north. Innes-Taylor's quiet land was being opened up by developers, but he did not stay home long enough to watch all the changes.

His specialized knowledge of cold weather survival was as sought after in peace time as in war time. In the early 1950s, many of the major world airlines started flying the polar route between North America, Europe and Asia. Inevitably, they turned to Innes-Taylor for help.

"I trained all the pilots of the Scandinavian Airline System, Air France and KLM (Royal Dutch) in Arctic survival techniques," he said. "We had survival schools in Scandinavia, France, Holland, and Alaska, and we always took the pilots into actual field conditions, as well. Actually, the air crews loved it; they got a real kick out of it. It's very fortunate there hasn't been a forced landing of a commercial airliner on the sea ice," he said. "But if it does happen the pilots are prepared for it."

Innes-Taylor has lived in Dawson City and several other places along the Yukon River, but in recent years he has made Whitehorse his base. He does a lot of consulting work for the federal government and other agencies which have their offices in the capital.

In 1962 he was involved in bringing history to life in the form of entertainment, as the general manager of the first Dawson City Gold Rush Festival. The festival was an ambitious plunge into show business and an artistic success, although plagued with financial problems.

Much of his work is involved with historical research, and this led him to embark on yet another new career when he was in his late sixties. American and British film makers arrived in the Yukon, and Innes-Taylor was hired as a consultant. He guided a U.S. television crew down the Yukon River for a documentary and then gave technical assistance to the English film maker David Cobham while he was making a movie of Jack London's story "To Build a

Fire." Cobham was so pleased with the Yukon setting of this movie that he returned to the territory in 1972 to film the story of the Mad Trapper—the crazed.gunman who led the RCMP on a long cross-country chase in the N.W.T. and the Yukon in 1931-32.

"I even played a part in that film—I'm the trader," said Innes-Taylor, who found the whole business of film making a fascinating experience.

As a very private man, Innes-Taylor gave only the bare bones of a reply to a question about his family. He has a wife, Elizabeth, and three grown children. His eldest daughter is an archivist at the University of Alaska, his son teaches English at the University of Tokyo, and his younger daughter is considering a career in journalism.

The only subject on which Innes-Taylor became expansive was the environment. This thoughtful man was roused to passion when he talked about the mess that civilization has brought to the wilderness. He is convinced that the preservation of unspoiled areas of the world in their natural state is essential for the sanity of man.

"Man needs a place for reflection in these times," he said. "And that can only come from being isolated from people for a while. People scream when they can't surround themselves with radios and other noise, but I think the peace of mind available in the wilderness is one of man's greatest values."

His name has often appeared in northern papers as a champion of conservation. If there is such a thing as an ecology freak in his seventies, then Innes-Taylor is that man. As long as he is alive the Yukon will have a capable and articulate defender of its unpolluted lakes, its wilderness parks, its Himalayan-type mountains, its flower-filled valleys, and its beautiful wildlife.

Chapter 9
Louis Mero
Man-of-all-trades

British Columbia is too young to have had much of a history, but a lot of high adventure has been packed into the more than one hundred and eighty years since the first white man set eyes on B.C. There have been Indian wars, gold rushes, huge fires, epic railroad construction and daring exploration into some of the wildest country on the face of the earth. And with such exciting events have come men of independence and fortitude. B.C. has produced many men who became legends in their own lifetimes.

Louis Mero of Hazelton claimed that he knew two of B.C.'s truly legendary characters, the packer Cataline and the Indian fugitive Simon Gunanoot. Mero's recollections of Gunanoot are particularly exciting, because they do not echo the official version.

Mero, who was ninety-three when he died in 1975, lived in a huge, two-story home on a slight hill at the top of a meadow, surrounded by forest. The hand-lettered "no trespassing" sign marking the start of the trail across a creek and up to the old house seemed out of place, because Mero was always happy to see a visitor.

Across the horizon, dominating the scene, stretches a chain of mountains, so high they are nearly always tipped with snow. There is 5,775-foot Nine Mile Mountain and the Rocher de Boule Range, towering 8,000 feet.

Mero's house was located four miles up the Skeena River from Hazelton, near the Indian village of Kispiox. This land, where the Skeena and the Bulkley rivers meet, is among the most romantic in B.C. for its scenery and its legends. In winter, mist swirls low over the tree tops and the beautiful totem poles of the Indian villages. It is no wonder the native people of this country tell fantastic stories and carve them with such feeling into the wood of their totems.

The Carrier Indians, who lived on the banks of the Bulkley, were known as the quiet people. And they were talented, as well as peaceful. Long before the arrival of the white man, the Carriers spanned the river with poles lashed together with cedar ropes. This bridge was considered a marvel of primitive engineering and, when it was later reinforced with wire by the crews of the telegraph line, it served for half a century.

Mero came to this wild land in 1903, after working his way across the country from his home in northern Ontario. He was of French descent, but said he was raised in a German community.

Mero's independent spirit drove him to leave his home and the warmth of his family—his parents and nine brothers and sisters. He moved from Ontario to Manitoba, Saskatchewan and Alberta, working all the time on railroad construction.

Railroad construction brought Mero to B.C. in the first place, but that was not the work which kept him in the west. He began prospecting when he reached the mineral-rich rivers of B.C. and saw much of the province that way. However, luck was not with him or the men he backed with grubstakes.

"I spent ten thousand dollars on that prospecting, what with one thing and another," said Mero. "Grubstaking is what beats a man. You don't know whether they are getting grub or whatever with the stake and you are getting nothing out of it. I grubstaked four men one summer, and that kind of set me back."

Mero decided to try ranching instead. After looking around, he settled on a place about four miles from Hazelton. "I've got one hundred and fifty-six acres—it was supposed to be a quarter section, but I'm four acres short, and I don't know how that came about," he laughed. To acquire clear title to his homestead, he had to build a structure on the land, and he started on a 24 by 22 foot log cabin.

At the same time that he was setting up his ranch, Mero fell in love. His choice was a French-Canadian girl with the English name of Fanny. He was working in Hazelton when he met her, and she was employed at the local brothel. In Mero's words she was "waiting at table," but local people of that era had no hesitation in describing her, in the vernacular of the time, as a "sporting lady."

Whatever she was doing in the Hazelton brothel, Fanny stayed there only a month before Mero, in his words, "snapped her up." And from that moment on, no one could have guessed Fanny's previous occupation. She became a devoted wife, as faithful and hard working as any husband could wish.

The couple were married in Hazelton in 1910 and at first lived in Mero's town cabin. "I didn't have over a thousand dollars when we got married, but that's the way it goes," he said. "We lived in town, because my ranch didn't have no door on it. It had no windows or floor or anything like that." These minor details did not bother Fanny. She was determined to move out of the town cabin and picked a bitterly cold day in February 1911 to do it.

"She just got up one morning and said to me, 'Let's go out to the ranch, Lou,'" recalled Mero. He protested that the snow was two to three feet deep, but Fanny shrugged off this fact as not worth worrying about.

"Well, you'll find out before you get there," warned Mero. So Fanny fed her husband lunch, bundled up in some thick clothes, and the two of them headed for the ranch. They got there all right, lit a fire in the stove, and had a cup of tea. Mero thought the trip would satisfy his wife, but he had underestimated her.

"When we got ready to go back," related Mero, "she said, 'We'll move out tomorrow.' 'Not in this,' I said. But she just said 'Yes, boy, right in this.'" And she got her way.

Next day, Mero borrowed a team of horses from a friend and moved all their belongings from town to the doorless, floorless ranch. Meanwhile, Fanny rented out their town cabin for $20 a month—astonishing her husband, who never dreamed she could get such a huge sum for the place.

"Then I went down to the sawmill and got a load of lumber and inside a week we had a swell place at the ranch," said Mero. "She fixed up the other cabin and sold it for four hundred dollars and then her and I went a-cutting cordwood."

The newlyweds were determined to be ranchers. "We cleared all this ground here," said Mero—indicating a vast expanse of meadow, a vegetable plot, and one solitary rose bush surviving from his wife's gardening days. "All we had was an axe, a saw, and a stump-puller."

The homestead along the Kispiox Road soon earned a reputation for its ever-open door, as Mero and his wife were lavish with their hospitality.

"Anybody was welcome to their house, anybody at all," recalled their one-time neighbor, William (Billy) Dunn.

"People never went up and down the old Kispiox Road without stopping in at Mero's—it was just the most natural thing to do. Both he and Fanny were very fond of the bottle, of course, and Fanny was quite a character. They were a natural pair, ideally suited to each other, and there was never any conflict between them. Their only fault, if you can call it a fault, was their fondness for booze."

Dunn said that in 1912, Mero was a short, powerful man, almost as wide as he was high, with a thick black beard that jutted out. As for Fanny, Dunn said she became the "perfect wife" after she married Mero and the only thing that marriage did not change was her language.

"She talked like a man and cursed and swore and spoke her mind," he said. "But she had a heart as big as a bucket and no better woman ever lived for kindness and generosity. And she was as good as a man at anything—she could drive a wagon and work like a slave."

Mero was proud of his wife's ability to work like a man and she helped him greatly with his hauling and packing jobs to bring in extra cash to operate their ranch. "You bet she came with me," he said. "She freighted and cut cordwood and collected her own money. My wife had a team of horses and so did I."

At this time, Mero became acquainted with Cataline and Simon Gunanoot, both famous B.C. figures. In those days, the ability to pack vast quantities of goods was more valuable to a man than intellectual skill, and Cataline was the best packer in B.C. Cataline, whose real name was Jean Jacques Caux, was born a Basque, but left Europe for western Canada in the 1860s. Soon, his mule trains were plodding through the wilderness at ten miles a day, as they carried supplies to mining and construction camps, telegraph crews, settlers and trappers, from Yale to Ashcroft.

According to Art Downs, in his book *Wagon Road North*, Cataline was a broad-shouldered man with a barrel chest and a slim waist. He quickly became known both for his tremendous strength and his honesty and reliability. He was an unusual sight in the bush because he always wore a boiled white shirt to which, on special occasions, he attached a collar. Around his neck, he wore a silk kerchief. Downs wrote:

> A distinguishing feature was his shoulder-length hair. His favorite drink was cognac and he rubbed a little of each drink on his hair, considering this ritual as a preventative for baldness. As he massaged the liquor into his scalp, he would say, "A little inside and a little outside." He was a friend of the Indians and never once in half a century of packing did he have trouble with them. Another reputation of which he was proud was that he never failed to fulfill a packing contract. On two occasions his mule teams were virtually wiped out, but his freight was delivered—on the backs of Indian women he had hired to carry it. When freight wagons made packing to Barkerville unprofitable for mule outfits, he simply moved north.

Time eventually caught up with Cataline. His mule trails became roads, and his exploits legends. He made his last trip in 1913, ending a career of fifty-two years. When he died in 1922 in Hazelton, the town where he had often wintered during his packing days, he was believed to be at least eighty. He is buried on a high bench overlooking the country he knew so well.

Mero became friends with Cataline because the packer spent so much time in Hazelton. He got to be part of the scenery—sitting on the hotel veranda with a big black dog at his feet.

"Cataline was the best packer there was," said Mero—and he knew what he was talking about, because he himself did quite a bit of freighting with teams of horses. "He was a good old soul and he was a friend of mine, though he couldn't talk English very good. He had a language of his own, half French and half English, and it didn't make any difference whether you understood him or not. But most of us around here could understand him. It was a sight to see him go by with his pack train—he had a hundred mules in one train."

Mero recalled how people new to the country were always surprised at how fast the pack trains could travel. "They went by a horse a minute, two men to the horse, three hundred pounds on a horse. Why, that's nothing for a horse. We've had men here who have packed three hundred pounds. And women, native women. In the early days, that's how all the freight went from here into Manson Creek.

"A man had to go a hundred and eighty miles with that freight—from here to Slave Creek and then to Manson. I don't know how long it would take. They would make so many miles a day, and tea-up and rest up a couple of hours and keep a-going."

Mero often saw a man carrying a 300-pound load, and he knew a man who carried a cast iron stove on his back all the way from Hazelton to Manson Creek—right over the Omineca Mountains. "Those men got seventeen cents a pound for packing, so the more they packed the more they got," said Mero. "Of course, a lot of people think that's horrible. They can't believe it, but it had to be done. Those packers packed everything—machinery, groceries, dry goods."

The second B.C. legend who was a long-time friend of Mero's was the Kispiox Indian, Simon Peter Gunanoot. Gunanoot's story started in 1906, with a brawl in the roadhouse at Two Mile, a tiny community two miles from Hazelton. Two Mile had always had a bad reputation. Gunanoot, who was a well-known hunter and a powerful man over six feet tall, had just returned to his native village of Hagwilget after a successful winter on his trapline. He went to the roadhouse to celebrate with his brother-in-law, Peter Himadon, and there they got into an argument with two half-breeds named Alex McIntosh and Max LeClair.

The argument was about the morals of the Kispiox women, so feelings ran high. Gunanoot left the roadhouse to get his rifle. A few hours later, the bodies of both half-breeds were discovered. They had been shot through the heart, while riding their horses. This marksmanship indicated that the murderer was a crack shot, as Gunanoot was known to be.

"I knew Alex McIntosh well, and he had it coming to him," snorted Mero. "Everything was wrong with him—drink as well. Whoever shot him made a good job of it. Nobody knows if Simon shot him and the other fellow or not. They have no proof for it." Many people agreed with Mero, but the police had to do their duty.

Both Gunanoot and Himadon fled before an inquest was held. They each knew the country north of Hazelton and it was easy for them to vanish. At the inquest, only Gunanoot was cited as the killer, but Himadon chose to stay with him. Police patrols searched in vain for the two fugitives. According to some people, Himadon eventually died on the trail, but year after year Gunanoot lived his hunted existence and was eventually joined on the run by his wife and children.

The family lived in a 14 by 10 foot tent, which was never pitched more than two months in any one place. There were eventually eight children—at least one was born in the bush while Gunanoot was a fugitive and one died during those years. The family had caches of food and ammunition spread through the country between the Stikine and Skeena rivers and they packed their tent and gear by dogs in winter and on their backs in summer. Gunanoot continued to trap, and he disposed of his furs through friends, who kept him supplied with food. And every year, the police went searching for him.

At this point in the story, Mero's version differed radically from the official one. According to Mero, virtually everyone in Hazelton knew where Gunanoot was and could easily have led the police to him. However, the B.C. government paid high wages to the local men to act as guides for the police patrols, and they had no intention of ending such a good deal.

"They worked the B.C. government for about ten years on that and it cost the government a lot of money," said Mero. "The government would get a gang together and away they'd go—and they knew where Simon was all the time. They could have got him, but they never did, because the government was paying them good money. Six or seven fellows from here went up in a gang like that. The last fellow got two thousand dollars and he knew just where he could put his hand on Simon. That was the kind of government we had—every year they handed out money because they were going to get Simon. Why, I'd have paid Simon to stay out there—it would have been worth it.

"I remember I was out here in front of the house one day, cutting wood, and I see Simon coming up the road. He sat down and I said to him, 'Did you see the gang up there, Simon?' 'Yes,' he said, 'I seen 'em all. I just walked around them and come out.' "

Mero must have spoken the truth because one of Gunanoot's sons recalled years later that his father used to come and go in Hazelton, even when he was on the run. David Gunanoot, the son who was born in the bush, said his father disguised himself slightly to go into town, because he was eager to see the moving pictures. "He change himself," said David explaining how his father changed his clothes. "Then he go out to Hazelton and sit in that place, see that picture. He comes back, he tell us lots about it."

The younger Gunanoot was convinced that his father was guilty of the murder charge, all right, but the charge was never mentioned in the family camp. "He was a quiet man. Big, quiet," said David Gunanoot.

Eventually, the police admitted their inability to outwit the fugitive and decided to wait him out because they figured, quite rightly, that he would finally give himself up. But Gunanoot remained free for thirteen years. According to David Gunanoot, his father announced that he was going to surrender himself to the law with the words, "If they want to hang me, they can hang me up."

Gunanoot hired a well-known criminal lawyer, Stuart Henderson, who agreed to take the case because he knew there was money in it. After several meetings with Henderson, Gunanoot walked into Hazelton with his family in 1919 and surrendered. Duchie Kline, of the B.C. Provincial Police, reached a gentleman's agreement with the fugitive. He put Gunanoot in a cell as the law required, but left the door open so he would not get claustrophobia.

Mero disliked Henderson and his devious ways. "I knew Henderson for years, by golly, and he was an awful card," said Mero. "He cleared Simon, but he must have made pretty near six thousand dollars out of it, and Simon could have walked out of here any time."

According to Mero, Gunanoot told Henderson that a local merchant, C.V. Smith, owed him between $1,500 to $2,000 for furs. "The merchants weren't supposed to buy any fur from Gunanoot or supply him with any goods," explained Mero. "So Henderson walked in on C.V. and said, 'Which would you sooner, pay three thousand dollars or go to jail?' And that Henderson had an awful face on him, when he looked at you in a certain way. C.V. didn't know what to do or what to say, so Henderson just turned his back on him. And, by golly, C.V. wrote out that cheque because Henderson had him by the neck. He shouldn't have supplied Simon."

When the time came for the trial in New Westminster, Henderson pocketed C.V. Smith's guilt money, plus a fat fee from Gunanoot, to make a total of about six thousand dollars, if Mero's information is correct.

Gunanoot was acquitted in 1920 and lived until 1933, although he was ill for years with tuberculosis. He died in the bush, where he had trapped and hunted for years, and was buried at Bowser Lake like his father.

There were not many white people in Hazelton when Mero first lived there. A few prospectors and miners, a couple of merchants, a minister, and that was about all. The town expanded fast, with several hotels, banks, a hospital and a drug store, although its main population continued to be Indians.

"I never had no trouble with the Indians—everyone got along fine with them," said Mero.

"At that time, the Indians didn't like paper money. You couldn't give a bill to an Indian. They wanted silver or gold, because they could put it in a can and bury it and it would still be good. A lot of Indians kept their money buried in the early days and, in time to come, when they dig up a reserve, a lot of them tin cans will be pulled up."

The building of the Grand Trunk Pacific Railroad down the west side of the Bulkley River and on down the Skeena was a hard blow to Old Hazelton. The new townsites along the rail line were called South Hazelton and New Hazelton. The population of Old Hazelton dwindled over the years, but it never died.

The Grand Trunk Pacific was originally intended to be a second transcontinental railroad—a monument to the Liberal government, as the Canadian Pacific Railway was a monument to Sir John A. Macdonald's Tories. The railway was built in several different sections and the western portion was constructed from both ends simultaneously. The Pacific terminus was settled on as Kaien Island, where Prince Rupert is located, and the route chosen in B.C. was down the Bulkley to the forks of the Skeena and then on down the Skeena. Progress was slow because of construction problems, and the line to Kitselas on the Skeena was only graded by March 1910. The trains were operating to Skeena Crossing by March 1912 and in August 1912, the first train reached Sealy, often called Sealyville. This town, which no longer exists, was very close to Hazelton.

In 1913 the tracks were laid through the Bulkley Valley and on to Burns Lake. On April 5, 1914, east and west met near Fraser Lake, and the last spike was driven. By

1922 both the Grand Trunk and its rival the Great Northern were in financial difficulties and finally, the federal government took over them both to form the Canadian National Railway. So the Pacific coast terminal became Vancouver and the line from Jasper to Prince Rupert was a branch.

This railroad construction was the background to life in the Hazelton area when the Meros were married, and it brought all kinds of new people to town.

Mero spent most of the First World War mining for tungsten, which was in great demand because it is used, with other substances, in the hardening of steel. He worked in the Red Rose mine on Rocher de Boule Mountain, which he could see from the door of his home. Several of his friends joined the U.S. army and urged him to do the same, but his reply was always, "I'm a Canuck, boy, and I'm dying a Canuck." Mero was on the verge of enlisting in the Canadian army when the war ended.

In 1921, Mero gave up the ranch and went into the cedar pole business full time. He said he retired from it in 1946, but his old friend Dunn saw him still cutting poles at the age of eighty-five or eighty-six, so Mero was at it for at least forty-five years. This area of the Skeena Valley is famous for the quality of its cedar poles, which are used for telephone and telegraph lines and in railroad construction. Mero's poles—and he must have cut many thousands of them—were used all over B.C. and some were even shipped to Washington State.

"If I'd have stayed with the cattle, instead of contracting for cedar poles, I'd have been way ahead," he said. "I didn't make no money with the poles; it was impossible to make anything."

Mero had a crew of up to thirty-two men who worked for him cutting poles and when horses were still being used to haul the poles, he had anywhere from four to twelve head. After the poles were cut they were spilled into the Skeena in the spring and floated down river to Kit-wanga or Cedarville for collection behind a boom. Then they were hoisted out of the water and stacked beside the railroad for loading on flat cars.

"I'd ride a pole for miles on the river and I can't swim a lick, no sir, I can't make a stroke, even though I was raised right on Lake Huron," said Mero. "I fell off a pole once or twice, but that was nothing. I don't know why the river didn't get me and I've drove on all kinds of rivers." He wore rubbers on his feet, because the cork-soled boots used by loggers in eastern Canada would have worn out in a day on the rocks of the Skeena.

Driving a hard bargain was an essential part of life in those days, and people enjoyed a tussle of wits. Mero liked to recall how he got the better of a man named Scotty MacRae, who once sold him a horse for $80. He took the horse to his camp, where he was cutting poles, and had used her for a month when MacRae suddenly reappeared and tried to pretend he had merely loaned the horse instead of selling her. Apparently, MacRae wanted the horse back to impress his prospective father-in-law, who was making up a team of horses and needed one more good animal.

"You see, Scotty had told his father-in-law he owned a horse at my camp," said Mero. "He was the finest liar in the country, but that was one time he got caught."

Mero had no wish to sell the horse he had only just bought, but he agreed to part with her for $100—take it or leave it. Moreover, he also refused to walk the horse back into town—Scotty would have to do that himself. MacRae gulped, swallowed his pride, and wrote a cheque for $100.

Finding a cook for a remote work camp in the bush was always a problem for Mero. The men preferred a Chinese cook, but they were particularly hard to come by, because they were in such demand. Whenever Mero had a cook crisis, he would go home and say, "Mum, you'll have to come and cook." And Fanny, always the business woman, would reply: "All right, what are you paying?" But after a few weeks Fanny would get fed up and insist she had to go home to find out how far the cattle had strayed.

Mero's world fell apart in 1956, when Fanny died of cancer. He said her illness cost him every dollar he made, because she had to stay in hospital for nearly four years in Vancouver. After that, Mero carried on alone in the rambling old house that was murder to heat and had no running water.

"What do I want with water in the house?" he asked. "I've got two of the best creeks in the country, one on one side of the house and another on the other side. You can't get water like that in the city—it comes right out of the mountains. I can put it into the house any time I like. But you people in cities have it too easy. I pack my water, and in the winter I go down to the creek just the same, and just chop a hole in the ice and dip her up."

What with packing water, cutting wood, and trying to control the smokiest stove for miles around, Mero in his nineties was still a busy man. When he had his last three teeth removed at the age of ninety, the doctor wanted him to go into hospital for a few days for a general checkup. But Mero turned down the idea as ridiculous.

"I've no time for that," he said. "I've got a dog to feed and a house to look after."

Chapter 10
Andy Anderson
Logger

Logs are Andy Anderson's business. He has been a miner, trapper, sawmill operator, house builder, real estate dealer, and herbalist. But logging has taken up most of his time, and his knowledge of the forest industry is encyclopedic.

Anderson lives, appropriately enough, on the West Coast where the big trees grow. Powell River is his home—he has watched and helped it develop since 1908. In fact, he supplied the wood for sixty-two of the community's first houses.

The history of Powell River and the company which keeps it alive, MacMillan Bloedel Ltd., are interwoven with Anderson's life. The names of the founders of the pulp and paper industry in Powell River slip off his tongue with the ease of familiarity. He has known them all, worked for some, and fought with others.

And yet Anderson, who is proud of going broke four times and always bouncing back, is not a company man. He is a loner, an individualist. Even in his eighties, he is a maverick who relishes a battle of wits with city council or a big business executive. And Anderson is never at a loss for protagonists. He is also never without a joke—usually at his own expense.

"I'm growing down now, like a cow's tail," said the bent old man who was once six feet, two and a half inches tall. "If I bend over any more I'll be walking on all fours."

But his hands were still huge and his wrists as strong as steel bars, a legacy of the days when he could lift 200 pounds right over his head. He would never part with his belt and spurs, the tools of his high rigger's trade. "I won't sell them," he said. "I'll use them yet."

Andy is Anderson's nickname. He was christened Amandus Ephraim when he was born into a doctor's family in Sweden in 1882, and he is very proud of those Biblical names and of his huge family of brothers and sisters.

Dr. Anderson had fourteen children—ten boys and four girls—by his first wife. Then, when she died, he married again and had nine more children, plus three whom he adopted. Young Andy was only four years old when the family left Sweden for the U.S.

"We all helped on the ranch—we had to start milking cows when we were seven years old," he said. "We milked a hundred and twenty head at one time and it was all done by hand. There were no milking machines in those days. We had all kinds of cows when we started out, but later it was mainly Guernseys.

"We raised all our own feed, our own grain. Then we took the grain to be stone ground by water power. We had rye, buckwheat and wheat."

Anderson ran his first trap line along a river that

followed a short-cut route to school. "When I saw there was money in furs, I began raising skunk, mink, coons, fox, weasels and muskrat. I started the first fur farm in Wisconsin and sold to a furrier in Oshkosh. Even twenty-five to thirty dollars was a lot of money in those days. I shot porcupines to feed my animals."

But the fur farm was not well received by Dr. Anderson, who felt it was taking the boy away from his ranch chores, so he instructed the foreman to set the animals loose. "That's when I left home," said Anderson. "I was fourteen."

He had thirty-five cents when he left. He lived in the woods all winter in a trapper's cabin, packed in his food more than thirteen miles, and shot three bobcats for bounty. In March he was discovered, and his father ordered him home. But he walked out again several other times before he finally left for good at the age of sixteen.

Anderson got his first job, thanks to a surveyor friend, near Cold Lake, Alberta. "We surveyed them townships around Cold Lake—there were no settlers in there then," he said. "And that same winter I went trapping for the Hudson's Bay Company around Spirit Lake, Alberta."

The company was not willing to give the teenager a trap line at first, because they thought he was too young and fresh off the farm. "They thought I'd never stick it out, but I showed them," said Anderson. "I didn't have to learn trapping, because I'd done it in Wisconsin. But it was a tough life trapping in Alberta at sixty-five below. And the trappers, mostly French Canadians and half-breeds, were the toughest people I've ever met.

"In September we'd get our rations, our freight canoe, and a dog team and away we'd go. We didn't come out until May. The cabins were already built along the trap line and the rations was beans, salt pork and sow belly six inches thick. There were long slabs of it and it was covered with brown spots. You got no butter, no lard. There was not much variety, but lots of beans.

"But we did have a good choice and quality of meat—moose and deer. All you could eat, and you fed your dogs with it, too. There were geese and ducks before they took off for the winter and I had cords of them piled up for when I wanted to eat them."

Anderson spent only a year in Alberta, however, because one day he read about British Columbia in a magazine called *Hunter, Trader and Trapper*. "After reading that, I figured B. C. was going to be where I would end up. So I went to Edmonton and got a train for the Kootenays," he said.

Anderson arrived in B. C. around 1901, and started logging about six miles from Nelson. The logging job developed into a contract with the Weyerhaeuser Company (now called Weyerhaeuser Canada Ltd.) to supply big draft horses to haul logs. With some money and a place to spend it for the first time in his life, Anderson began to show the high spirits of a young man. Before he took on the Weyerhaeuser contract, he went timber cruising (evaluating stands of timber for species and volume) with a partner who had more talent as a clown than a logger.

Hammond (not the man's real name) was a little too fond of a drink, and most people in the area would not hire him anymore. "So I picked up with him and we went off to look over this timber," said Anderson. "When we were a ways from camp, we saw this she bear with two cubs—a black bear, you know. I had no gun with me, it was down below at camp, so I threw rocks at her and she chased the young cubs up a tree."

Anderson yelled at Hammond to run back to camp and grab a gun, while he stayed to make sure the cubs did not jump out of the tree. "But instead of just bringing the gun, like I told him, he brings the whole damn crew, about twenty-five men," said Anderson. "The she bear got scared with all these fellows and went around a bluff. I took a shot at its head and missed, but I was determined to get those two cubs up the tree."

There was little sentiment in those days—particularly from tough, young loggers—about separating a mother bear from its cubs. Anderson wanted a pet bear cub and that was all there was to it. Nothing was going to stop him. He scrambled up the tree after the cubs, with a snare quickly made out of a leather belt.

"They went higher and higher, and pretty soon the top branch was only about three inches thick, and I got scared to go any farther in case it broke," he said. "One of the cubs got so far out on the end of a limb that it started to bend and I tried to snare him but couldn't. So I hit him on the head and he fell down into the creek.

"I hollered at the fellows to catch him or throw a coat over him, because he was only small. But they were scared, and he got away from them."

The next thing Anderson knew, the mother bear was climbing the tree after the remaining cub and it was a race to see who would succeed. "I was thirty feet up in the tree tops and I sure was scared. That damn bear would have got me if she could."

But the loggers shot the mother bear out of the tree, and Anderson managed to snare the terrified cub and bring it struggling down to the ground. Anderson named the bear Mike, and it followed him everywhere.

The wildest of many episodes Anderson had with the bear took place in Nelson, when Hammond persuaded him to go with him to the Orangemen's Day parade in July. The crazy day began as the men waited for the train to take them to Nelson and ran into a group of Sons of Freedom Doukhobor women parading naked in one of their frequent religious protests.

"Gee, they are big, husky things those Doukhobor women," said Anderson, who had obviously been astonished by the bizarre scene. "Their breasts stuck out and they teetered up and down. They looked straight ahead, not at us, and there wasn't a stitch of clothes on them.

"I know some of them are strong as a logger. I saw

some of them pick up rocks and run with them to the wagon when they were hauling rock for a contract at the planing mill."

In Nelson, Anderson fashioned a chain out of hay-wire for Mike and led him around like a dog on a leash. The men checked into the Lakeview Hotel and Anderson persuaded the manageress to let him tie the bear up in the backyard for the night. All would have been well if it hadn't been for Hammond. On this particular night, Hammond's big joke was to take the bear down to Nelson's red light district, while Anderson was asleep.

"I didn't know the first thing about it until afterward," said Anderson. "Hammond was drunk, and he took the damn bear down to see the girls. While he was fooling around, the bear took after one of the nigger wenches, scratched her all up, and tore her clothes off.

"At eleven-thirty that night there was a rap at my door and a policeman asked me where the bear was. I said it was tied up in the backyard. But I didn't know Hammond had taken the bear away to the red light district, then brought him back and tied him up again."

The only thing the policeman knew was that he had his man and his bear, and he led the two of them off to jail. So Anderson and Mike spent the rest of the night in separate cells in the Nelson jail.

"Next morning I thought I'd get a fifty or hundred dollar fine, but all I got was a ten dollar fine and two-fifty in costs," said Anderson. By then he was a minor celebrity in town.

"So I led the bear down the street, with the dogs barking after him, and tied him up again," said Anderson. "Every day I was in trouble over that damn bear. The kids would come to see him and the hotel was fillled up with kids all the time. The hotel owner got after me and the bartender got after me. So I gave the bear away to the shipyard."

Mike did not stay long in his new home and Anderson never found out what finally happened to him.

In 1908, after spending some time working for a mining company, Anderson came to Stillwater, which is about twelve miles south of Powell River near the present B.C. ferry terminal at Saltery Bay. He cut ties with a broad axe for a railroad and witnessed the beginnings of a huge pulp and paper industry.

The founders of the industry in Powell River were three Minneapolis men—Dr. Dwight F. Brooks, his brother Anson S. Brooks, and Michael J. Scanlon. These timber brokers, who ran one of the continent's largest logging and sawmill operations, saw the potential of the Powell River area as a site for a pulp and paper plant. They bought the holdings of the Canadian Industrial Company for $330,100, merged with a local man named O'Brien, and formed the Brooks, Scanlon, O'Brien Company.

In 1909, these men incorporated the Powell River Paper Company with a capital of $1 million. Eventually, their empire stretched from Canada to Florida and even to the Bahamas. Brooks and Scanlon died in 1930, and thirty years later the company they had founded merged with MacMillan and Bloedel Ltd. to become MacMillan, Bloedel and Powell River Ltd. Finally, in 1966, the words Powell River were dropped from the company name and MacMillan Bloedel Ltd. was born. Now the company is the largest forest industry firm in Canada and the Powell River unit is the largest of its operations.

However, when Brooks and Scanlon began operating in B. C. in 1909, there was not a single newsprint or pulp mill in Canada west of the Great Lakes. Demand for newsprint was increasing and the colossal firs and cedars of Powell River were an obvious attraction. So a dam was built across the narrow entrance of Powell River, which is only three-quarters of a mile long and is claimed to be the shortest river in the world. By 1912, the plant was in production and by 1913, the four-machine mill was in operation, and a

25,000 horsepower dam had been built. In the early days of the mill, all except shiftworkers had a sixty-hour week.

A tug and two scows shipped in the logging camp equipment, and a railway—probably the one on which Anderson worked—ran from Powell Lake to the saltchuck only a few miles away. The first logging was done by oxen; later, horses were used, and then "steam donkeys" (portable engines attached to a winch) were brought in. Anderson claimed to have used the first steam donkey in operation in B.C.

The community of Powell River was named after a pioneer doctor, Israel W. Powell (1836 - 1915), who was a consistent supporter of the movement that led B.C. into Confederation in 1871. Powell River, in 1914, had a company store and a dance hall, but it was still not much more than a clearing in the bush. Anderson has seen the town grow from a population of forty to its present total of about nineteen thousand.

"It used to take us five to six hours to walk the trail from Powell River to Stillwater, because of all the windfalls along the way," he said. "We'd often find a guy out stiff lying under a tree with a bottle beside him. And sometimes we weren't much better off ourselves, after they opened a saloon at Powell River."

In 1909, Anderson went to work for a logging operation in Campbell River for a while, but it was not long before he was back in Powell River. He found a job with the Michigan and Puget Sound Lumber Company, which was logging on Powell Lake by means of the railroad to the coast. The southern end of the thirty-two mile long lake is only a mile or so from Powell River and the ocean.

"They dumped their logs right where the paper mill is now," said Anderson. "They came down under the bridge and along the river, and dumped the logs by a switchback. In those days you just backed up against shore and pulled in the logs.

"The guys I worked with were from all over the

place, but mostly they were Indians. And Jim Springer was running the camp there." Springer, a famous pioneer character, had started logging in the Powell River area in 1883 with oxen.

By a strange chance, Anderson knew the founders of the Powell River Company through his father. Dr. Anderson and Scanlon had become acquainted in the eastern U.S. and the company also had medical connections through its other founder, Dr. Brooks.

"It was a help to me," said Anderson frankly.

Like so many other men in B.C. at the start of the century, Anderson tried his luck at gold mining, but only succeeded in losing more money than he made. When there was a gold strike on the Tanana River in Alaska in 1912, he was talked into providing a $500 grubstake for a friend who was keen to try mining. But the friend let some others in on the deal including "a ballroom woman who was running a dance hall" and Anderson ended up with only a quarter interest in the little 100-square-foot claim.

When he took a boat to Alaska to see what was going on, he found the ground still frozen and no work being done on the claim. "I just fooled around up there—I didn't know anything about mining," he said. "There was gold there, all right, but by the time we got down to bed rock it was June and the freshets came in and filled up all our holes. So we sold out to the Guggenheim family and didn't get much gold. When I arrived back in Seattle, all I had was fourteen dollars—I lost all my grubstake."

Anderson also took part in two small gold rushes in B.C. at Zeballos and Manson Creek, but was unsuccessful and soon returned to logging. But he was proud to be the nephew of the famous Klondike miner, Charlie Anderson—otherwise known as the Lucky Swede.

This other Anderson was thirty-seven at the time of the Klondike and, after an all-night drinking session, he woke up one morning to find he had bought an untried claim for $800. Angry at himself, he reluctantly started work on what he thought was a worthless claim and found himself mining $1 million worth of gold and earning himself the tag of the Lucky Swede. But luck ran out on him in the end. As Pierre Berton relates in his book on the Klondike, the Lucky Swede's dance-hall-girl wife divorced him after spending his money on travels around the world. The San Francisco earthquake laid waste to his wealth, because he had invested heavily in real estate. He ended up pushing a wheelbarrow in a B.C. sawmill for $3.25 a day, but he remained an incurable optimist until he died.

Anderson was both a high-rigger and a chaser in his time. A high-rigger was the man who rigged the spar trees—the trees to which lines were attached to pull in the felled logs. A chaser was the man who unhooked the logs that were yarded in to the spar tree. In the early days of logging, the work was even more dangerous than it is today, because it was less mechanized, and Anderson saw many accidents.

"I've packed eighteen injured men out of the woods in my time," he said. "One company killed seven men in a week and the Workmen's Compensation Board shut them down. They had a bonus racket on, so much a log, and the logs were moving pretty good. The fellows tried to work too fast with this bonus and that's when the accidents happened.

"I got sick of rigging and I would take any job. So I was chasing one day and the fellows were fighting hang-ups [trees caught in other trees during falling]. As I came along I got the signal to go ahead, but instead of the logs jumping away from the hang-ups, they pulled this big snag down," he said.

At the time Anderson noticed one of the loggers heading off the trail, but did not think anything of it until much later. "I was running the same road practically all afternoon, fighting hang-ups, and I noticed that when I went by the big tree which the snag had pulled over, a cloud of blowflies would come up—it was August then," he said.

When the shift changed, the men noticed the chaser was missing and began to look for him. Suddenly, with a horrible premonition, Anderson remembered the blowflies he had seen during the long, hot afternoon. "We went back to look and there we spotted him—dead under the snag," he said. "We had to cut an eight-foot hunk out of the tree to get him out."

This frantic pace in the woods took place during the First World War and the loggers made a lot of money. But after three or four years of high wages—for those days—a slump set in very suddenly.

"I took awful chances myself, but I never got badly hurt, just slightly," said Anderson. His accident happened when he was acting as second rigger, the logger who wires up the spar tree after the high-rigger.

"I saw this big burl on the side of the spar tree," he said. "I gave the rigger the signal to drop me, he let the line roll full speed, and I went to take a kick at the burl and missed it. I landed on my hip and couldn't walk for three weeks. So I quit; to hell with that, I quit."

In the First World War Anderson was called back to the U.S. for military service, "but when they found out I was logging airplane spruce, they said it was essential work and sent me back.

"I never experienced anything like that airplane spruce," he said. "You had your choice of the best of the log. If it wasn't just right, you cut the butt off and then you cut the best piece off. Sometimes you only got a sixteen-foot log out of a big tree.

"All the rest of the logs—I had quite a boom there—were sold for twenty-eight dollars a thousand. There was a sawmill here on the lake and the mill bought the logs from me, sawing and shipping them. There were about two hundred thousand board feet altogether.

"We'd put the logs in the rivers and then the freshet would come and the logs would get into the beaver meadows and sloughs. I'd put some of them into the rivers half a dozen times before they got to Powell Lake. In some places, they had to come two miles down the rivers to the lake. The biggest log I ever put in was twelve feet and four inches. That was a Douglas fir. And I put in several cedar that went twelve feet."

Although Anderson logged at various places up and down the coast, he spent most of his working life on Powell Lake. "I was always pretty well on my own," he said. "When I saw an opportunity I'd take a contract."

Anderson was working on Powell Lake when he met his wife, Clara. Throughout their life together, they have had a very close relationship. Whether it was on the trap line, packing a deer out of the mountains, or driving a logging truck, the two of them were a team.

Clara, in her old age, is not in good health, but her tongue and spirit remain lively. She broke both knees in a fall off the porch when she was about eighty and after that accident, had trouble moving around. "The doctor said she wouldn't walk again, but she did," Anderson said. However, Clara remained housebound from then on, and he did the shopping.

Anderson was as proud of Clara's Scandinavian background as he was of his own. Her parents came from Norway originally, emigrated to the U.S., and moved to Canada when she was a teenager. "Her father was a Viking," said Anderson. "And his grandfather or great-grandfather was the inventor of the compass."

Clara was living in a float house on Powell lake when she first met Anderson. Most of the occupants of these float houses were loggers; Anderson himself lived in one for about ten years. "She was in the kitchen cooking for the men most of the time," he said. "Then she'd leave for a while, and she was here, there, and all over.

"Poor old widow," said Anderson affectionately—his wife was divorced from her first husband when he met her. "I told Clara she shouldn't marry me. I was never cut out for a married man. I'm too much of a roamer. But she talked me into it." In a way, it was a business deal as well as a marriage, because Anderson needed someone to take care of the clerical work of his logging contracts.

Clara said she did all the office work and the trucking. "You couldn't waste time then, let me tell you," she said. "I came back from the sawdust deliveries and the lumber truck would be ready to go out. After that I'd take out a load of wood, and I was a crack shot, too."

Her husband confirmed every word. "She's hauled millions of feet of lumber," he said. "She used to be really strong, and we did a lot of hunting together. She'd climb mountains and pack out a goat or a deer. As an outdoors woman, you couldn't beat her. She was one of the best."

Anderson even took Clara out with him on his trap line and told her if she did not like it she could go home and stay home. "But she was a sticker—she stayed right with me," he said.

Anderson dated the main events of his life from the work he happened to be doing at the time. So he knew that he and Clara were married when he was building Powell River's golf course in the mid-1920s. "Part of the golf course used to be the old graveyard and the graves had to be moved," he said. "I cleared two hundred and eighty-five acres for the golf course—logged it first, because it was heavily timbered. It was a big job, but I didn't make much money at it. I still have some of the old bull shoes I found when I was making the course. They had been logging there with bulls in the old days."

The Powell River Company, which employed Anderson to build the golf course, also contracted with him to clear the land for the present townsite. "I logged and cleared it and sold the logs on the open market," he said.

At one time he owned sixty-two lots in Powell River, because of what he called "a credit deal." He supplied the lumber and all the construction materials for the houses he built for the company. "And then we wound up with all the profits in lots," he said. "You had to take what you could get."

The Depression was rough on Anderson, as it was for most British Columbians. But he struggled on with his logging and sawmilling. "You could get the best of men to work for fifty and sixty cents an hour and they'd be pestering you for work," he said. "Logs dropped in price from sixteen dollars and fifty cents to six or seven dollars a thousand in just a few months. There was just no market. You couldn't make a dollar, so I went broke."

Going broke was a familiar experience for Anderson by then so, as usual, he picked himself up and started again. This time, he concentrated his efforts on Powell Lake. In 1932, he started his sawmill on land leased from the Powell River Company because he was stuck with sixty million feet of timber that he could not sell. He stayed in the business for twenty-eight years, owning his own sawmill and planing mill.

"I bought three sawmills to make one and sold what was left over," he said. "My sawmill was just around the bay at the south end of the lake—they call it Anderson's Bay now. Between the camp and the sawmill I'd have twenty-five to thirty men working for me.

"I've had lots of ups and downs. Sometimes the market would jump up and labor didn't follow, and you'd think you was going to be a full-fledged logger. Then all of a sudden, labor would be up and logs were dropping."

In about 1960, the company cancelled Anderson's lease and he had to move the mill—which was worth $78,000—to its present location beside his house. But the mill never worked again, because the municipality would not let Anderson run a commercial operation from the new site. It became a very sore point with the old logger, who so desperately wanted to be in business again.

One of Anderson's many jobs in the past had been working at a distillery, where he learned how to make whiskey. He later became the best winemaker in Powell

River, using blackberries, cherries, loganberries and parsnips. Blackberry wine was his specialty, but Clara would not drink it if it was more than two years old.

"I drink a quart of rum and a gallon of wine every week," he said. "A lot of old-timers say it's the wine and snoose that keeps me going. I use snuff a bit, but I quit smoking about sixty-five years ago—it got my wind, you know. I couldn't climb the hills."

One of Anderson's great interests was herbs. He once took a course on herbs and picked up a great deal more about their uses from Indian friends over the years. "I used devil's club bark thirty-five years before it ever got into a drug store," he said, referring to the bark of the prickly shrub called devil's club that grows in backwoods near streams and rivers.

"Once I got dysentery from eating too much meat on the trap line up in Spirit Lake, Alberta," he said. "Well, we used to get a gallon of overproof rum when we were on the trap line, and it was really strong stuff in those days, and I didn't like it. So I gave it to an old Indian who came around, and I told him about my dysentery. He said he would give me some Indian medicine and he brought me this devil's club bark. I've used it ever since. I'm never without it. It's funny that nobody gathers it around here."

Horsetails—plants that grow in moist soil along streams and rivers—were used by Anderson as a vegetable. "They were the finest spring greens you can get; you can hardly beat them and they carry vitamin B12," he said. "Lemon juice is another thing I use. To get rid of a bad corn, you soak a piece of toast or a crust in lemon juice and make a poultice. Then you put the poultice on the corn and, if you leave it on long enough, that corn will be gone."

He described his garden as "organic" because he used no artificial fertilizers, only ash from his wood stove. "There's no potash like burned wood ash," he said.

The wood stove in the Anderson household was used both for heating and cooking, because Clara could never adapt to an electric stove. "I put in a big electric stove—a real nice one," said Anderson. "Then I ordered the electricians in, but Clara wouldn't have it hooked up. She didn't want it."

Anderson is rounding out his days with a dispute of the kind that has haunted him most of his life. His property is the only privately owned land left on Powell Lake and the municipality would like to acquire it for park. But Anderson is not about to give up his home until he is ready. He also has sixty sections of logs floating in the lake, but he is asking more for them than the mills are willing to pay. So he can neither cut logs nor mill the ones he has. His sawmill is rusting into the ground beside his weather-beaten house.

Recent years have been frustrating for Anderson because he would like to travel, but he is anchored at home by an ailing wife, chickens to feed, goats to milk, a garden to tend, hay to cut, wood to chop, and a log boom to guard.

He bent down and patted his dog, Sam, who squirmed with pleasure. Then he took a sip of his favorite drink—beer laced with rum—and said he attributes his longevity to his dreams.

"I dream more than most people. Or maybe I just remember them better," he said. "I've studied my dreams and worked with them. When I was logging, if I had an unlucky dream, I wouldn't fall a log that day." But Anderson was always a very practical dreamer, as far as money is concerned. And he also has a very big heart.

"When I pass on, I don't know of any better place for my money than the crippled children and the old age pensioners," he said. "That's how my will is made out, and it's registered in Victoria. And Clara is figuring on the same thing as me. We want to take care of people coming along behind us.

"But I figure on spending a lot of it before I go," he said, smiling.

Chapter 11
Fred Engebretson
Rancher

Like many stories of British Columbia, this family saga
began in Norway. In 1867, Jakob Johnson left his childhood home there to try his luck in the new world. He
worked first in Wisconsin and then moved on to Minnesota
where he acquired a fine piece of land, edged by the Red
River that runs across the border into Lake Winnipeg, and
started farming. He married a Norwegian girl who was also
an immigrant, and they had three children. But within a
short space of time, two of the children and their mother
died. Johnson found himself a widower with one surviving
child, a five-year-old girl named Annie.

Until she was nine, Annie lived with her grand-mother. Her father, broken-hearted by the death of his wife and children, continued to farm, although he was reluctant to stay in the place that had brought him so much unhappiness. So he was very receptive to the excited talk around the state of Minnesota in the 1890s about the similarities between the coast of Norway and the coast of British Columbia. A Lutheran pastor from Minnesota went to look over B.C. and check into reports of a proposed railway. The pastor liked what he saw and heard, and began organizing a mass migration from Minnesota to B.C. The government in Victoria was willing to set aside the Bella Coola valley, 350 miles north of Vancouver, for a settle-ment, provided that a colony of at least thirty families was established. The government also promised that a wagon road in the valley would be built and that each settler would be granted 160 acres of land free as a homestead.

The colony which the pastor helped establish was set up to "induce moral, industrious and loyal Norwegian farmers, mechanics, and businessmen to come to Bella Coola." There was even a ban on liquor in the new colony.

The Canadian Pacific Railway did its part by reserv-ing two large sleeping cars for the trip and reducing fares, and the first part of the move was on. The men had to go first, of course, so twelve-year-old Annie was left behind with relatives in Minnesota when her father set off for B.C.

Johnson was one of the eighty-four settlers who went by train to Vancouver and then by steamer to Victoria, where they bought tents and provisions. On October 27, 1894, the settlers boarded the steamer *Princess Louise,* char-tered by the CPR, and three days later they arrived in Bella Coola. Led by their pastor, they went ashore in Indian canoes and landed about twelve miles up the Bella Coola valley.

This broad, lush valley, hemmed by mountains from six thousand to nine thousand feet high, provides a green pass through the Coast Range mountains. In 1793, the explorer Sir Alexander Mackenzie, the first white man to cross Canada, had ended his epic journey in Bella Coola.

There were only sixteen white people living there when Johnson and his fellow settlers arrived in 1894. Man had made scarcely any impression on the beautiful valley with its tall trees and fjord-like coastline so very similar to Norway.

The settlers drew lots for homesteads, so that the rich bench land, swamps, and forests were evenly divided. A few men soon turned back because the winter was so rugged, but the majority stayed on. The government allotted $10,000 for roads and bridges in the valley and the settlers started to work on a road.

In May 1895, the steamer *Danube* arrived with the wives and families of the settlers, and this is the boat that brought Annie, now aged thirteen and a pretty little blonde, to join her father.

"I was all alone on the trip, but the rest of the bunch looked after me," said Mrs. Annie Engebretson. "Then we got out of the boat into Indian canoes and they took us up the river to dry land."

By that time the settlers had hacked a trail along the twelve miles of the valley from the place where the steamer disembarked its passengers to where the colony's camp was established. But the trail was so rough it took two days to hike it and young Annie wondered what she was coming to after the quiet and civilized life of a Minnesota farm.

"B.C. looked very different from Minnesota, but I kinda liked it right away," said Mrs. Engebretson. "I was sickly all the time in Minnesota and I always had to take medicine. But when I got here I just left the medicine aside and started working and got all right. I got strong, you see, because we had a pack on our backs for three years on and off."

She lost count of the number of times she backpacked up and down the trail. The main settlement twelve miles from the sea was originally called Bella Coola,

Fred Engebretson
179

but it suddenly changed to Hagensborg after a store and some buildings were erected there by a man named Hagen Christensen. A settlement farther down the valley was called Lower Bella Coola. When a village grew up by the sea, it was also called Bella Coola, and all these names caused great confusion.

In November 1895, some more settlers arrived to bring the total colony up to 220, and the community has been growing ever since. But the original colony faced a great disappointment soon after it was established, because the promised railroad never materialized. At one time, Bella Coola was in competition with Burrard Inlet to be the terminus for the CPR. And at another time, four different railway companies announced plans to build a railway to Bella Coola. But nothing ever came of these early schemes, and the first settlers had to fend for themselves off the land. Luckily for the fish-loving Norwegians, they could not have settled beside a more productive part of the Pacific. With salmon up to fifty pounds and steelhead of more than twenty pounds, there was always a meal from the sea. But Johnson had no wish to become a commercial fisherman, as so many of his fellow countrymen later did. When he saw the railroad was not coming, he decided to try ranching in the interior where there were immense stretches of open land.

Johnson's family is not sure of the date when he first set foot in the Chilcotin country. Anyway, it was around the turn of the century when Johnson climbed up from the gorge of the Bella Coola River and reached the 15,000-square-mile Chilcotin plateau. Today it is still open grassy rangeland, occasionally cut by rail fences, dotted with lakes and meadows, and patched with forest cover. The plateau is a startling contrast to the narrow canyon of the Bella Coola River which is crossed by many creeks and filled with cathedral-like groves of huge fir trees.

The Chilcotin country abounds with wildlife, from

migratory water fowl to big game animals, and was a hunter's paradise when Johnson first explored it. There are about ninety-five miles between Bella Coola on the coast and the tiny community of Anahim Lake on the Chilcotin plateau, and Johnson walked all the way there and back. For many miles he cut trail with a tool called a grub-hoe, or mattock. The work was back-breaking, but he enjoyed the open country after the narrow coastal valley, and he took a good report home to his daughter.

"It was pretty wild country, but he liked it, and so he crown granted some land at Towdystan near Anahim Lake," said Mrs. Engebretson.

Towdystan is no more than a bend in the lonely dirt road, officially called Highway 20, that winds for almost 300 miles between Williams Lake and Bella Coola. Towdystan is halfway between Nimpo Lake and Anahim Lake and its population consists of one person—Fred Engebretson, who is Johnson's grandson and Mrs. Engebretson's elder son. Fred Engebretson, a confirmed bachelor in his sixties, is known as the mayor of Towdystan. He still ranches on the 640 acres that were staked by his grandfather.

"It's the oldest surveyed place in the whole country," said Engebretson proudly. But that is the extent of his pride in the little ranch he runs, because he considers the countryside totally unsuitable for cattle.

"If you tried to figure out why people came here in the first place, you'd almost give up," he said. "In modern times you'd send people to Essondale if they tried to ranch here, because it's a ridiculous place to come. It's really bad land for ranching. But there was big talk in them days about a railroad coming through, so everybody wanted to grab land. They were just speculators, not ranchers, those people. No rancher in his right mind would come here today, but it's great speculating country."

In spite of Engebretson's negative feeling about ranching in the Chilcotin country, many have tried it and succeeded. There are ranches right across the plateau, and

Fred Engebretson
181

the colossal Gang Ranch, a million acres before some of it was sold in 1973, is just one of them. Certainly Engebretson's grandfather was no land speculator. He loved horses and cattle and that was his sole reason for moving there and starting to ranch. And in his small way he succeeded, too.

Mrs. Engebretson attended school regularly when she lived in Minnesota, but she never went in B.C., because she was far too busy helping her father. "I tried to look after him and I started to cook, but at first he could cook far better than me," she said. "My father had to be both mother and father to me and I helped him as much as I could."

Although she got no further regular schooling in Bella Coola, she always went to Sunday school, walking four miles there and four miles back. She walked because one day, when she had gone on horseback, her horse ran into a wasps' nest, threw her off, and bolted. "The wasps were just as thick as could be and, oh boy, I got stung," recalled Mrs. Engebretson. "After that I always walked to Sunday school."

In the early days in Bella Coola there were no horses to help the settlers, and all the packing of goods had to be done by manpower alone.

"It was two years before they got a horse," said Mrs. Engebretson. "Finally, the pastor went out and bought a horse and wagon and started hauling the stuff that way. Before that, I remember my father and some other men packing a stove into the camp. It was a tremendously heavy stove and they got some Indians to take it sixteen miles up the river against the stream. But then the Indians left it on the river bank, because they didn't want to pack it any further. So my father and uncle and some other relatives took turns to pack it on a stretcher."

In 1903, Johnson felt he had had enough of life in the valley and, with his daughter, decided to move to the land he had crown granted in the interior. But he still hung on to the more than one hundred acres he had in Bella Coola.

"We went on horses all the way to Anahim Lake—to our place at Towdystan," said Mrs. Engebretson. "It wasn't easy riding, because you had to go up a six-thousand-foot mountain. It took the horses all day to get up. In fact, it was easier to walk."

As for the Bella Coola River, cattle swam it and people paddled across in an old Indian canoe provided by the provincial government. Johnson took three cows with him from Bella Coola to Towdystan and he was given a lot of help from Indians along the way.

The Bella Coola Indians are short in stature and belong to the Salish nation. They are surrounded by tribes with whom they have no linguistic or biological connections, such as the Chilcotin Indians, who tend to be tall and athletic. But to Mrs. Engebretson they were all "good and very helpful Indians."

Johnson built a log house on his land at Towdystan and gradually developed the property into a small cattle and horse ranch. The only animals he disliked were sheep and he refused to have them on his ranch. All his supplies had to come the hundred-odd miles from Bella Coola and that meant horses all the way. One year he packed in a mower, rake and sled on horses across the mountains. "He had several men helping him and it took them eight days," said Mrs. Engebretson. "One horse had over three hundred and fifty pounds on his back, so they could only go a short distance every day."

She was twenty-one when she moved with her father to the lonely ranch near Anahim Lake, but she rapidly adapted to life in the wilderness. In the winter of that year, she rode across country some sixty miles to the tiny community of Chilanko Forks just to pick up mail. "We hadn't had any mail all winter, so I wanted to go," said Mrs. Engebretson. "I took a saddle horse and rode there all by myself and camped out at night on the way. The coyotes bothered my horse so much in the night that I had to get up and chase them away. I had a gun, but I didn't want to shoot them.

They're cowards, you know, and they run away when you chase them."

There was an Indian trail to the ranch and a handful of cabins that made up Chilanko Forks, but Mrs. Engebretson preferred to go across country because it was quicker. "It was hard to find the way, but I made it," she said. "And on the way back, I went through in one day—but it was a long day."

Johnson had to drive his cattle to Chilanko Forks to be sold every year, and Indians helped him with this drive, while his daughter stayed home and looked after the ranch.

When she was twenty-six, Annie Johnson married a man whom she had known for a long time—a farmer, Thomas Engebretson, who had originally come from North Dakota. "I couldn't get married before that because I had so much work to do," she said. "My husband was more of a farmer than a rancher, but he liked cattle and horses just like my father."

The couple were married at Towdystan by a visiting parson and then stayed on there with Johnson to run the ranch as a family business. They were busy all day, every day.

"My father made furniture with a cross-cut saw and my husband was pretty handy too," said Mrs. Engebretson. "They sawed all the lumber for the roofing and the floor of the house we built. I made all my own clothes by hand—after a while I got a sewing machine—and the men bought overalls for a dollar fifty a pair. And they were good overalls for that money, too.

"We had kind of a little store at Towdystan. Everybody had at that time, because if you had a surplus of goods the Indians would buy it. We took both fur and money from the Indians. We didn't know much about furs, so we often got stung.

"But we got to be very good friends with the Indians. Once we went to Bella Coola for three or four weeks, leaving the door open by mistake, and the Indians went by and locked it and never took anything.

"I wasn't lonely because I had too much work to do. But we didn't have enough to read and I like reading. And, of course, there was no radio then and no telephone at first."

The family divided their time between Towdystan and Bella Coola, because they had homes in both places. They headed for the coast as soon as the mosquito season started in early June. The horses were so glad to escape from the insects that they raced for the mountains as soon as they were given their heads. Toward the middle or end of July the family returned to the interior and then made another trip to Bella Coola in the fall to stock up for winter.

"We took ten packhorse loads of supplies up from Bella Coola for the winter, so we never ran short of food," said Mrs. Engebretson. "Ten horses could take a ton, and sometimes we made two trips."

The first of Mrs. Engebretson's five children—a girl—was born in Towdystan in 1907. "An Indian woman came and helped me and I didn't see a doctor because there wasn't one," she said. "The Indian woman knew all about it—'For three days you don't do nothing,' she told me. She looked after the baby and everything. If you are friendly with the Indians, they'll do anything for you.

"I generally had my babies in July in Bella Coola and I'd ride down there on horseback to have the baby," she said.

By 1916, Mrs. Engebretson had three small children and no way to educate them, so the family moved back to Bella Coola and the ranch was rented out. Johnson stayed with his daughter, while Engebretson found a job as a packer with a survey crew in the north of the province. By this time the small school built by the settlers in Hagensborg in 1898 was inadequate, so the men of Bella Coola set about building a new school. "They done pretty good, but it wasn't much of a school," said Mrs. Engebretson. In 1920, Jakob

Johnson died, and Thomas Engebretson took over his late father-in-law's ranch. As the children left school one by one, the family resettled in the Anahim Lake area. The eldest girl died as an adult, but the four younger children are still living near Anahim Lake. The married ones have given Mrs. Engebretson ten grandchildren and twenty great-grandchildren.

As the elder son, Fred Engebretson was destined to inherit the ranch eventually, but he was in no hurry to do so. He is never in a hurry to do anything and he does not believe in making any hasty changes. The house where he now lives is crammed with the belongings of three generations.

Fred Engebretson took up the family story from the year 1925 when, as a teenager, he first started fishing in Bella Coola. His younger sisters were still going to school there and the Towdystan ranch was rented out.

At that time Bella Coola consisted of three or four stores, and the local population fished and trapped or worked in the fish cannery or the one sawmill. Men like Engebretson rented a boat from the cannery and in 1925 about ninety-nine per cent of the fish boats were sail.

"So you didn't have no pollution problem and whatever you made you took home," said Engebretson. "It was easy fishing in those days, just like a vacation. Nobody cared to make a million and everybody was happy. We just went out when we felt like it, just like a bunch of kids. There were lots of fish and we never fished far out, so the water was always calm. We fished three or four months in the summer and then, in the winter, there was nothing to do except cut wood. And I trapped a bit.

"I fished commercially from 1925 to 1939 or 1940," he said. "They were good years for fishing, but poor prices. We didn't get much more for a whole sockeye than they do per pound today. The last year I fished, we got thirty cents a piece for a sockeye and two-and-a-half to three-and-a-third cents for pinks. They wouldn't even take all the chums or dog salmon—they just took the brightest ones, because they were overloaded with fish.

"I fished right through the Depression. Nineteen twenty-nine was a good year and I probably made two thousand dollars, but in 1930 I probably didn't make a hundred dollars. There were no unions, you see, and in those days there were stone age laws. You couldn't even buy a job and there was no welfare. You could hardly afford to have any land because the dollar or two extra for taxes was too much. But we were young then, so we didn't mind, and no one seemed to starve because of the fish."

In 1932, Engebretson returned to the Towdystan house and began ranching again but, until the end of the decade, he always went back to Bella Coola in the summer to go fishing. "It was the only way of making a dollar," he said.

Engebretson had to start from scratch again on the ranch, because the family's fifty head of cattle had been sold when the place was rented. "I bought about ten head at first and kept building up from there," he said. "But I still don't have many—a hundred head at the most now. With labor problems, it's pretty hard to afford any more. So I do a little bit of everything—cattle ranching, trapping, running a sawmill. Oh, there's lots of work and there's ten miles of fence to look after."

Engebretson used to drive his cattle 100 miles west to Bella Coola to sell them and at least once he drove them the 190 miles east to Williams Lake. "That drive would take about three weeks because you could only move about ten miles a day, as the cattle would be feeding all the way out," he said. "Three or four ranchers would have a hundred and fifty cattle, all together, and that would be about an average drive. You'd lose hardly any cattle on a drive like that because they got used to being driven after three or four days. And the government had holding corrals every ten miles, so you could put them in there for the night and you wouldn't lose any.

Fred Engebretson
187

"In the morning you'd turn them out and let them eat a while and then start trailing another ten miles. So it wasn't much of a job, but it was slow. The drive started about September first and in them days there'd only be a couple of thousand head sold at the Williams Lake sale. Nowadays they sell that many in one day and all the cattle come in by truck. But in the early days some of the big ranchers drove their cattle all the way to Kamloops and that took two months or more."

Engebretson, like many men in the Chilcotin country, has spent most of his life on a horse. Horses are necessary in every aspect of his life today and they were even more important in the past. He now has about seven horses, but at one time he had three or four different teams of work horses. Before the road went through, the nearest doctor was 100 miles away across the mountains in Bella Coola, or 112 miles across the plateau in the opposite direction to Alexis Creek. Engebretson once did the Alexis Creek ride in winter, through two feet of snow, to get a man with a broken leg to a doctor.

"They started off with Ed in the evening and got here at dark, so I joined them and we got about thirty miles and then changed teams on the sleigh," said Engebretson. "Every ranch would lend us a new horse, so that we could keep on going to Alexis Creek. It took about three days traveling steady, because you could only make about five or six miles an hour. But we made it and no one died from lack of a doctor that I know of."

The government's telegraph trail to Bella Coola was completed in 1913. It was packed in on horses from Bella Coola to Tatla Lake and was joined at Tatla Lake by the trail coming from the opposite direction. This line gave the Engebretson family the luxury of a telephone.

"The telephone company used to call me whenever there was a break in the line and ask me to ride out and find it," he said. "It was a twenty-mile ride in one direction and twenty-five miles in the other direction. It would take me a full day to find the break, but then all I had to do was tie the two ends together."

For forty years, Engebretson had a trapline, and that and his fishing experience have given him first-hand knowledge of the ways of wildlife. What concerns him most is the way it is slowly disappearing. "There's one salmon now for every hundred there used to be and one duck for every thousand there used to be. I don't know if it's because of the increase in human population," he said. "There once would have been a thousand wild horses between here and Chezacut, sixty miles as the crow flies, but there was a hard winter in 1934 and ninety-five per cent of them died.

"In the old days, you'd never go a day of the year without seeing a moose from the house. You didn't have to go out and hunt them, because they were right there. Between here and the creek   [a distance of about fifty miles] you'd see five or six every day. Now there is no feed here, so the moose have moved to higher range."

Engebretson said wolves used to go around in bands of twenty or thirty in the winter, but now he has not even heard them howl for twenty years. "I have never known a wolf to attack a man," he said. "I've trapped them, but they're not easy to trap. They are smarter than a coyote and they're good to have around because they keep the mice down."

Like so many trappers, Engebretson shot down some of the long-held myths about animals, such as the one that wolves will only attack the weaker, poorer animals. "That may apply to moose but not to sheep," he said. "A wolf will attack the healthiest sheep. There was a she-wolf here once that killed about twenty of my sheep one fall. I saw her and set traps, but I just caught coyotes and the wolf saw that and got elusive."

The current practice of putting out forest fires as fast as possible is something that Engebretson deplores. "In this area, you should burn ten per cent of the land every year to improve the game," he said. "When we first came here we tried to burn all year, but we couldn't do it. We hunted every two weeks or so and shot a moose or deer to eat and we'd be twenty or thirty miles away from the house. So if we thought we could get a fire going we'd set one, but it never worked. I never did get one to work and I've only been here for fifty years. But I haven't tried for thirty years now, because I could go to jail, I guess. And the forestry people are flying around looking for fires all the time. But in those days it was different, because this land was considered of no value, and the forestry people didn't care."

Engebretson said he usually tried to start fires in June, because the hay crop might have accidentally burned up in an August or September fire. "And if it burned up your hay, you were through," he said.

When forest fire fighting became government policy throughout the province, Engebretson was startled to find himself given the job of a local fire warden. He was only to be paid when he worked (when there was a fire to put out) so, obviously, the authorities did not know of his inclination to reach for matches.

"I had to go and hire Indians to fight the fires and they'd get mad, because they had started the fire in the first place," said Engebretson. "One Indian said to me, 'I've tried for fifteen years to burn this trash and now I've got it going I've got to put it out.' So the Indians didn't like putting out fires, but they liked to get paid. They knew what they were doing when they tried to set fires. They were making better range for the deer and moose."

Engebretson said the only fire fighting equipment used in the early days was a shovel and an axe—"and it's some of the best equipment you can have." With these tools, he said, a twenty to thirty-acre fire could be put out in two or three hours "if you hit it just right." He added: "But if there's a wind blowing all night and the fire gets away on you, then nobody can stop it, even with the modern equipment like airplanes they have now."

Engebretson likes a drink these days and his hospitality is famous around Anahim Lake. But he swore that he never drank more than one and a half bottles of liquor and a dozen beers in total until he was over thirty.

"When I was fishing, it was all you could do to make enough to buy grub instead of liquor," he said. "It took a whole day's pay, then, to buy a bottle. Forty years ago, people would have starved to death trying to eat the way we do now. We ate mostly meat, because there was lots of animals. But through the winter we didn't have butter or milk or anything like that, and we made our own lard. You'd just eat moose meat and beans, that was the staple diet. And bannock and sourdough hotcakes."

When food ran out, two or three men would get together and take a sleigh into Bella Coola. Later on, when the road was passable for rugged vehicles, one truck load of food would arrive in the fall with enough to supply most of the ranchers all winter. Nowadays, four or five trucks a week come in loaded with food.

"It would take that one truck almost a week to make the trip from Williams Lake," said Engebretson. "If you got in a mudhole it would take longer than a week. Of course, some people still packed their stuff in with horses or a sleigh even after the truck came in."

Hunting has given Engebretson some of his most memorable moments in life and they have ranged from trying to shoot film of grizzly bear to the more deadly kind of big game shooting during a crazy expedition to Africa.

The hunting with a camera usually took place about a hundred miles north of Towdystan in the company of a Vancouver furrier, now retired, named Rudy Pop. Pop, who had a wooden leg, was addicted to bears. At first he shot them with a gun, but later switched to a camera, and he would go to any lengths—as Engebretson found out—to get a good bear photograph.

"We thought we'd fly in with a live sheep and use it as bait," he said. "We had it hog-tied on the airplane and we

Fred Engebretson
191

took it in alive to a big slide on a high mountain and that saved us from having to pack it in dead."

That was the plot, but it soon misfired. It was noon on a hot day—exactly the time when a bear is least likely to appear—so Engebretson put his rifle down as he and Pop pulled and pushed the sheep on a steep hill.

"Just then a grizzly charged us," said Engebretson. "It came running right at us, but we just stood our ground and I pounded a rock with my long-handled axe. We were mad; we'd been working with this sheep and we didn't want any interruption. If a bear charges you, your best bet is to stand your ground, not to try to run or climb a tree, because when the bear gets about six feet away from you, he is pretty scared too. You have to stand up to them, there's nothing else to do. And that's what we did and it worked. The bear decided to leave us. The sheep was the most scared of all. It was roped and tried to get away, but we had ahold of it."

A few drinks started Engebretson's trip of a lifetime to Africa in the early 1960s. He and a millionaire friend who often hunted in the Chilcotin had talked for years about taking a trip to Kenya. Then, one night, they decided it was now or never. "I was drunk before I left and I never quit drinking when I got there," said Engebretson ruefully. "That trip cost me ten thousand dollars. To do a thing like that you've either got to be a millionaire or a darned fool, and I guess I was the fool."

He and his friend spent six weeks in Kenya shooting an average of four or five animals a day, mostly wildebeest, which is a variety of large antelope. "We'd just shoot them and strip them a little bit and let the jackals and vultures eat them," said Engebretson. "You had to do that, otherwise the jackals and vultures would starve to death, and they needed those animals to do the cleaning up. There were too many animals there at that time and they had to shoot them off. We saw a hundred and fifty thousand animals in one day, we figured, and at least half a million in all the time we were there."

Engebretson takes great pride in his knowledge of the Chinook Indian language, even though he admits he has forgotten much of what he knew as a younger man. "I still can't really talk it, you know, but I understand what they are talking about, which they don't like much," he said. "They always learn you the dirty words first and they've got more of them than we have in English.

"The Indian language changes quite a bit, even in fifty miles. There is no rhyme or reason. It's not like any other language that I learned. They always put the noun in front of the verb. Like if I asked them if they had seen my horse, I would have to say, 'Horse, have you seen mine?' Everything goes like that. We call them Chilcotin Indians here. Then the Bella Coola Indians can't speak any language that even comes close to this one."

Engebretson said many B.C. names of lakes, rivers and mountains resulted from white men trying to imitate words spoken by their Indian guides. For example, he said, Towdystan is an English version of the Indian word for liquor and probably came about when a white surveyor pointed to the water of a tiny lake nearby and his Indian guide responded with the word for liquid or liquor.

"It's the same with Chezacut; that's very like an Indian word," said Engebretson. "The surveyor probably pointed at the lake, but the Indian guide thought he was pointing at a bunch of geese that were molting, and the Indian word for molting geese sounds just like Chezacut." He said that there are many lakes with names such as Tatla and Tatza which sound very like an Indian word meaning hello, voice, or noise.

There is one mystery of Towdystan that Engebretson thinks he will never solve, even though it has intrigued him for years. It involves a man, now dead, named George Turner, who came to the Chilcotin from the U.S. Engebretson is convinced that Turner, who died in Kleena Kleene in the late 1950s or early 1960s, was involved with the notorious Dalton Brothers—a gang of Kansas bank robbers of the

Fred Engebretson
193

1890s. In 1914 or 1915, he witnessed a near death struggle between Turner and another mystery man.

According to U.S. history books, five armed bandits attempted a double bank holdup in Coffeyville, Kansas, in 1892. The residents of the town heard the cry of alarm from the banks and turned their guns on the gang. Within twelve minutes four of the gang were dead and the fifth, Emmett Dalton, was badly wounded. A sixth member of the Dalton gang escaped, because his horse had gone lame as he rode into town.

Emmett Dalton received a life term as a result of Coffeyville, but he was pardoned after fourteen and a half years in the penitentiary and eventually died in Los Angeles in 1937. Engebretson is convinced it was Emmett Dalton, not long out of jail, who suddenly showed up in the Chilcotin to settle an old dispute with the mystery man named Turner who had arrived in the country from the U.S. several years previously.

Engebretson was about five years old when the confrontation took place at Towdystan. For six months or so Turner had been very fidgety, as though expecting something to happen. In those days, Turner often stayed at Towdystan for a few days during his travels in the Chilcotin and he was there the day a man suddenly rode up to the Engebretson log cabin and pulled out a six-shooter. Turner immediately reached for a double bit axe and ran out to face the newcomer. A blood bath seemed imminent.

"This old house was built like a fort, you know, with three feet of rock work around," said Engebretson. "So us kids had to lay on the floor in case bullets started flying, because that's what it looked like and everyone had their guns loaded in the house. We don't know how it ended, because no one went out, but they were shouting at each other and then this other guy took off. In them days it was good country to hide out in because you could cross the border without anyone knowing. There was no police to speak of."

Engebretson often talked to the mysterious old man, who had a reputation for honesty, although he also had a very bad temper. Apparently Turner once admitted that he had known a man who had half his face blackened from a gun blast, and that confession reminded Engebretson of Blackface Charley, who was once a member of the Dalton gang.

"Turner died with his secret, at any rate," said Engebretson. "I guess the fellow who came in here figured that Turner still had some of the loot, because they had been robbing for years. But if he did, I never saw or heard of it. He didn't throw it around.

"I don't like to say this, but I can't prove it and it would be impossible to check it out now," he said. "But when this old guy named Turner died—and he lived until he was about ninety—the police checked him over and said no doubt it was him who'd been tied in with the Daltons."

A little of B.C. history—that can be verified far more closely than the Dalton gang rumor—is still visible beside the road about ten miles from Towdystan. What can be seen are the remains of trenches dug by Indians during the Chilcotin war that ripped across this country for a few months during 1864 and claimed the lives of twenty white men. For several years before that, relations between the white men and Indians had become very strained, because so many native people had died from the smallpox and liquor brought in by white men. The war started in the spring of 1864, when Indians murdered a gang of road-builders at Bute Inlet. When word of the massacre reached Victoria, Governor Frederick Seymour set sail for Bella Coola on a fifty-one gun frigate, loaded with men and weapons, to round up the murderers. But in the meantime, the Indians had prepared an ambush for a white packer and killed three members of his pack train. This bloody ambush took place near Towdystan, at a place called Fish Trap Bridge, where the Dean River flows out of Nimpo Lake and across Highway 20.

Fred Engebretson
195

"The Indians dug three trenches about thirty feet long and about three feet deep and waited there for the pack train," said Engebretson. "The trenches are still there, but they are only about a foot deep now. Back in 1914, though, you would not dare to ride into them because they were still fairly deep."

Some of the Indians were eventually caught by Governor Seymour's armed patrols and five of them were hanged in August, 1864, in Quesnel. But the majority of the murderers escaped. The Indians who had lain in wait for the pack train at Fish Trap Bridge must have had their families with them, because Engebretson knew one man who had actually witnessed the massacre as a child. "He was only four or five years old at the time and he told me the fight lasted quite a while," said Engebretson. "He's been dead for more than twenty years now and he was about ninety when he died."

The road near where the ambush took place is the lifeline of the Chilcotin country. Its 300 dirt miles were once a caribou trail and its route has changed substantially over the years. The Palmer Trail was probably the first official name for what is now Highway 20; it was named after Lieutenant H.S. Palmer of the Royal Engineers, who surveyed it in 1862. Palmer was quite a character—he disliked horses and often went surveying on foot, with his men carrying all their equipment on backpacks.

Over the years the trail gradually became a road, but it wasn't until 1952, ninety years after the first survey, that construction started on the toughest section. This was the forty-eight miles between Anahim Lake and Bella Coola, and the route led right over a 6,000-foot mountain. It was a nightmare construction job, but the road was finally finished in late 1953.

But Engebretson figures the road is in the wrong location at Towdystan, because any brisk wind blows dust from the highway into his creek and kills the fish. So, to get his own back at the engineers who ignored his advice about the route, Engebretson gives misleading answers to all their earnest questions about the state of the creek. "They believe whatever I tell them," he said with satisfaction.

To Engebretson, who has no kind words for the country that is his home, the road brings little happiness for those who travel it. In his eyes, the Chilcotin plateau, where the January temperature can dip to sixty-five below, is a land fit only for real estate speculation.

"You can't compete with the prairies here," he said. "It's okay for rich people who like hunting, but that's it. There used to be a sucker born every minute—maybe there are two now. Strange characters always come in here. I guess this is the place where all the dissatisfied people come—they head for the end of the road."

Chapter 12
Albert Faille
Prospector

To describe a man as a legend in his own lifetime is a cliché of the worst kind and usually untrue. But Albert Faille was a legend and for once, the statement is absolutely true.

Faille, who died in 1973, spent most of his life on a fruitless search for a lost gold mine in the Nahanni country of the Northwest Territories. He lived years entirely alone there, in one of the wildest, most remote, and most beautiful parts of North America. The South Nahanni River flows through the fabled Headless Valley, marked on maps as Deadmen's Valley, which for decades has been a place of mysterious deaths.

In his more than thirty-five years on the river and its tributaries, Faille has had more than his share of close calls. He was attacked by wolves, suffered from scurvy, ran out of food, and swamped his boat many times. And above all, he escaped with his life from the Nahanni River, which so many others failed to do.

Faille was born in Pennsylvania, but he could remember little of his very early youth. "I ran away from home when I was a kid of about nine, but I don't remember why and I don't remember my parents," he said. "I was an overgrown kid when I was twelve, I was pretty near as big as I am now and I was strong. They didn't ask how old you were then, as long as you could do the job. So I knocked around doing jobs here and there."

Gradually Faille drifted westward and came to Duluth, Minnesota, on the western end of Lake Superior, about a hundred miles south of the Canadian border. "I was on and off into Canada trapping ever since I was thirteen years old," he said. "My district was between Fort Frances and Fort William, which is now Thunder Bay." That "district" covered more than two hundred miles of the border country between Ontario and Minnesota.

Faille claimed he never went to school and was eighteen when he taught himself to read and write with a little help from a "forestry guy." As he put it, "I'm fairly good at figures, but I'm no good at spelling. I read after I grew up a little bit, but I didn't have no time in the bush. I took a few magazines with me, but that was all."

Faille got married in Minnesota, but he and his wife, Marian, did not stay together long. "She was a city girl, a banker's daughter," he said. Nonetheless, for years Faille sent his wife all the money that was left each year after selling his furs and buying supplies.

In the First World War, Faille went overseas with the U.S. army to France. He served with the 10th Engineers in what he called a "forestry outfit" and spent most of his time cutting lumber and working in a sawmill.

Albert Faille
199

Faille reckoned he was in his early thirties when he first came to northern Canada. In 1924 he started trapping on the Beaver River north of Fort Providence, N.W.T.

The South Nahanni River rises near the Yukon border, drains two mountain ranges, then joins the Liard River, and finally empties into the great Mackenzie River. From its source until it joins the Liard at the foot of a bell-shaped mountain named Nahanni Butte, the river is more than three hundred miles of spectacular beauty with canyons, rapids, hot springs and waterfalls. It has canyon walls higher than the Grand Canyon and falls almost twice the height of Niagara. The Nahanni is a dangerous river of white water, jagged rocks, and swiftly changing channels, and is reputed to be the most treacherous and fast-flowing river in North America with an average speed of twelve knots. After one of the vicious wind and rain storms that often sweep the area, the river has risen as much as seven feet in an hour.

The Nahanni has long been a silent and deserted place where even the Indians seldom went. The lowland Indians were fearful of what they called the fierce Mountain Men Indians, who were believed to haunt the lonely high country. And so the Nahanni remained secure in its isolation. The romantic stories about the river even included a tale of a tropical valley set in the midst of Arctic wastes. The valley actually turned out to be five hot sulphur springs near the river, around which thick ferns grew and butterflies and humming birds fluttered in the summer—lush, but scarcely tropical.

Then in 1906 came the event that started the Headless Valley story and the rumors of a lost gold mine. The brothers Willie and Frank McLeod died in the valley while on a search for gold. Their skeletons were found in 1908, rolled in blankets in their camp beside the river. The mystery was that their skulls were missing. Their brother, Charlie, found the skeletons and became convinced the men had been murdered for their gold, because a message "We have found a fine prospect"had been left in the camp. There was no trace of the young Scottish engineer, Robert Weir, who had been with them. Charlie McLeod decided someone had shot his brothers through the head and then cut off the heads to remove the evidence. He was also sure his brothers had found a gold lode somewhere on a creek on the upper Flat River, which is the main tributary of the Nahanni. But in 1909, a skeleton believed to be Weir's was found, and the RCMP concluded that all three men starved to death. Only one thing is certain: the truth will never be known.

The valley where the dead brothers were found is eighty miles up the river and 1,000 feet above sea level. It is two or three miles wide, ten miles long and is ringed with mountains. Just before entering the valley, the Nahanni flows through an incredible canyon which knifes through the mountains for fifteen miles. Its towering rock walls rise sheer for 1,000 feet above the river, with mosses and dwarf trees clinging to narrow ledges. Set back by one or two slopes, the topmost cliffs stand 3,000 feet above the river.

In July 1927, the thirty-nine-year-old Faille headed toward the river for the first time. Albert Faille was on his way to see the fabled valley for himself. He had an outboard engine (what northerners call a kicker) at the stern of his freight canoe. Near the mouth of the river, he caught up with another canoeist poling his craft along. This man was also headed for the Nahanni and his name was R. M. (George) Patterson. The two became friends for life after this meeting, although they were destined to go in separate directions. English-born and Oxford-educated, Patterson wrote a book called *The Dangerous River*, which became the classic Nahanni story. This is how Patterson described Faille in his book:

> The Nahanni has probably never seen a finer canoeman
> and to watch Faille search out the weak spots in a riffle (a
> slide of water in a river) and plant his canoe's nose exactly

there, and neither to the right nor to the left by even a hand's breadth, is like watching a fine swordsman seeking for an opening, feeling out his adversary.

Patterson was headed for Virginia Falls, the 316-foot high falls about 130 miles upstream, and Faille was journeying to the Flat River, which joins the Nahanni about twenty miles below the falls. The Flat River was the center of all the gold stories, and even in those days Faille had gold on his mind. He intended to winter up the Nahanni and believed he would be the first white man in seven years to do so.

Faille and Patterson, seeing the river for the first time together, must have looked a strange pair. Faille was known as Red Pants by the Indians because of his homemade red wool blanket trousers. Patterson was far more dapper in drill trousers with a silk scarf knotted around his neck. In their separate canoes, they first tackled the Splits, some fifteen miles of treacherous water where the river rushes out of a canyon into flat land and divides into innumerable channels, sand bars, drift piles, and shingle islands. Here are found the notorious sweepers—trees that have fallen into the river, still clinging to the bank with their roots, lashing and beating at the water rushing by. The Nahanni is well known for undermining its banks and changing its channel.

After the Splits, the next challenge was Lower Canyon (sometimes called First Canyon), with its sheer walls and racing water. Faille got through with the aid of his three-and-a-half horsepower kicker, but Patterson had to do a lot of wading, pushing, paddling, and lining his canoe before he made it into Deadmen's Valley.

The men camped together, saw all kinds of animals, dined on bannock and moose liver, and had a great time. Always they were moving, sometimes together and sometimes apart. They navigated a place called the Second Splits (much like the first Splits) and then Second and Third Canyons. The going was tough, particularly when they had to portage the contents of their canoes to get the boats through a rough riffle.

The highlight of the expedition was Virginia Falls—a mountain of white water crashing down between rocky cliffs into clouds of spray and rainbows glittering in the sunshine. Faille was set to winter in the valley, but he accompanied Patterson down the river again as far as Twisted Mountain near the Splits. Before parting, the men stopped at the hot springs to bathe in the clear, blue water beside a meadow thick with grass, wild roses, and wild raspberries and gooseberries. Then it was time to say good-bye, Faille going up the Nahanni again and Patterson returning to his Alberta homestead.

"I built my first cabin on the Flat River in 1927 and I stayed up there for three winters," said Faille. Patterson revisited the Nahanni next year with his fur trader friend, Gordon Matthews. The men met up with Faille on the river in June 1928, and in *The Dangerous River* Patterson described his friend's first winter on the Flat River in these words:

> His trapline there was too much hemmed in by the moun-
> tains and on it he had nothing but bad luck. Early snow
> and ice caught him barely ready and then wolverines
> broke into his shack and stole three wolf pelts, and so
> much of his grub that he nearly starved. In order to get
> in, the wolverines tore out the stove pipe and enlarged
> the chimney hole and, once inside, proceeded to raise
> hell with the whole outfit. One dog was drowned and
> another ran away to the wolves. Faille himself slipped on
> a mountainside and was laid up for three weeks, during
> which time many of his traps were frozen into the over-
> flow ice, and he lost much fur. The game left the country
> and, being laid up, he was unable to follow or tell where
> the animals had gone; wolves and wolverine ate the fur
> from his traps; he fired at caribou, needing meat, and
> missed, not knowing that his fall on the mountainside

Albert Faille
203

had jiggered the sights until they stood permanently at 1,000 yards; he had some narrow shaves on a raft amongst the running ice, was wind-whipped by savage squalls and whirlwinds in the canyons on the way down—and his gold proved to be copper pyrites.

Most men would call it quits after a winter like that, but not Faille. He was back to his usual cheery self and keen to explore the country above the falls when he met up with Patterson again. And that was exactly what he did. As for Patterson and Matthews, they left the Nahanni in the summer of 1929 after surviving a dramatic winter at sixty below zero in a cabin in Deadmen's Valley. Patterson did not return to the Nahanni again until 1951, but Faille stayed on for forty-odd years.

He spent a brief period back on the Beaver River near Fort Providence and later, a few more years (he thought it was during the Second World War) as engineer on the Indian Affairs department gas boat *Thomas Murphy*. "We delivered the annual treaty money to the Indians along the Mackenzie and down to Fort Nelson, B.C.," said Faille. But most of the time he was trapping on the Nahanni and dreaming of the days when he would find the lost McLeod gold mine. "The Nahanni gold rush, people will say, Albert Faille started it." That was his dream. But Faille never found the mine, although he was always convinced it was there. "I don't think so, I know so, but where is it?" he asked. "That's a big, hard country up there and there's been mining and oil outfits and surveyors all looking around, but no one's found it yet."

Why did Faille persist with the fruitless search for so long? The answer may lie in a remark he once made to a friend, Colonel Harry Snyder, a Montreal millionaire oil man who did a lot of photography in the Nahanni valley. Snyder was pondering about the life of a prospector and said to Faille: "Some guy runs around all his life and never finds anything and some guy goes into the bush once and comes out rich." And Faille replied: "But look, Harry, at the fun you get out of it." So maybe that is what he was doing in the Nahanni all those years—having fun.

One of his toughest experiences in the early days was being frozen in on the Nahanni, because he accidentally marked the same month on his calendar twice. He was away trapping and thought he had lots of time to return by boat to his cabin, but when he reached the river it had already frozen. The problem was that the ice was not yet thick enough to bear his weight. "I had to wait until November fifteenth before I could get across to my cabin," he said. "I don't remember how long I had to wait, but I wasn't cold, because I was used to camping out. I had my gun, my axe, and my blanket with me, but that was all. It is sometimes more than fifty below in the Nahanni in winter, but you can always keep from freezing with a fire and I always had a good eiderdown bedroll. The thing to remember is don't sleep too close to the fire, or you're likely to burn your blanket up."

Dick Turner, who had trading stores at Netla and Nahanni Butte, and piloted his own plane around the Territories for many years, had been Faille's close friend ever since they met in 1934. His admiration for the man was unlimited.

"The most amazing thing about him is how he retained his sanity and his sense of humor after being alone for such long periods of time," said Turner, who is himself one of the most famous men in the N.W.T. Turner said most people who spend long periods alone in the bush usually become a little strange—they get suspicious of their neighbors or become convinced that someone is out to get them. "But not Albert—he's quite normal when he comes out of the bush, except that he talks a lot," said Turner. "It may have accentuated his independence a little, but he's always been very, very independent. He doesn't like to be helped in any way."

Albert Faille
205

In Turner's book, *Men of the True North,* he recounts his first meeting with Faille on a sandbar in the Flat River in May 1934. He caught sight of a "strange apparition with red wool pants, hair to his shoulders, and a long, red beard" who started talking even before Turner turned off the outboard. This, of course, was Faille.

> So help me, he did not stop talking for two days and two nights because he'd seen no other human for a year except Gus Kraus (another Nahanni resident) for a day or two in January. Two other men, Bill Epler and Ole Loe, were traveling with Turner, and they all spent the night at Faille's cabin at the mouth of Caribou Creek, a tributary of the Flat River.
>
> It was a clean, snug and well-built cabin with bunk, table, chair, door and windows. It was very neat and shipshape, as I found Albert's cabins always were. He loves the bush and takes great pride in his work. His cache was a small cabin built off the ground about twelve feet high to keep his supplies safe from scavengers, wolverine and bear in particular. The cabin had a dirt floor and Albert and Ole brought in great armloads of fragrant spruce boughs for a bed. Ole and Albert slept on these and Bill and I on the bunk.

Faille told the men that he had just come back from a disastrous trip to the head of the Flat River, where he had swamped his moose skin boat and lost everything except his matches, an axe, a pocket knife, and a frying pan half full of moose fat. The fat was the only food he had for the five-day walk and raft back to his main cabin on Caribou Creek. What's more, he lost a bundle of beaver pelts that were worth plenty even in those days. Faille said he had made the ill-fated boat out of moose skins and a frame of spruce poles in the manner the Indians had used satisfactorily for years.

Turner wrote:

> Albert left no doubt in our minds that that was the first

and last skin boat he would ever use. He was verbally vehement about it and used some flowery language to describe the lack of desirable features of all skin boats. I gathered that the most malevolent peculiarity of a skin boat was that when it shipped water it proceeded to sink and keep sinking.

After listening to Faille's tale of woe, the other three men agreed to go back up the Flat River with him to where he had seen a promising gold creek. They all piled into Faille's twenty-two foot freight canoe and headed up the river.

At the mouth of Irvine Creek, the men stopped to examine the ashes of a cabin, where a trapper named Phil Powers had died a couple of years previously. Powers' charred skeleton was found in the cabin and some reports stated that it, too, was headless, but the reports differ.

Up river, the men watched with admiration from the bank as Faille skillfully maneuvered the loaded canoe through a fast riffle, which they thought would defeat him. Wrote Turner:

> With the motor humming along, the canoe was just holding its own with the current. Albert stood up, reached for one of the poles, held the steering handle between his knees, and used the pole to push the canoe forward. At the head of the riffle the drop was a bit too much for him. He calmly laid down the pole, set the steering handle carefully, and stepped into the water. Working his way to the bow, he pulled the canoe up and over the drop into calm water. Then, with the kicker still humming along, he stepped back into the canoe and continued on.

The men portaged the canoe around the canyon of the Flat River along a trail that Faille had cut. Then they started panning for gold up several likely creeks, but had little success. Finally, they decided to head down river again and stopped along the way to go hunting. Turner shot one of the Nahanni's famous white Dall sheep and had a terrific struggle hauling it back to camp. But his friends would not eat it. As Faille put it: "An old ram in May is like a piece of shoe leather. That old beast is as poor as a crow."

At this point the expedition ran into a major disagreement—Faille and Turner wanted to continue prospecting, but the others wanted to quit because they were running low on tobacco. The men could not separate, because they only had one canoe. There was quite an argument, but Epler and Loe won. Turner explained why: "Albert knew from long years of experience and I knew instinctively that a disagreement among a party of men in the bush is one thing to be feared and avoided like the plague."

That trip was one of the few when Faille had company. Most of the time, he lived and traveled alone. "But I was never lonely on the river—I was always too busy to be lonely," he said. He also had his work cut out avoiding confrontations with animals. Many times he had a close shave.

"One day I shot at a bear while I was still in bed," he said. "I woke up and saw something sitting alongside my bed and I didn't have no dogs then. I noticed white under his chin and I knew it was a bear." Faille yelled, but the animal just sat there on its haunches swaying backward and forward. "His nose wasn't six inches away from mine and I reached for my gun, because I always sleep with my gun," said Faille. "The bear was just as surprised as I was, because he leaped up and ran and I missed him. I got up and fixed the fire, because it was time to get up anyway, and then I started to cook breakfast. And while I was cooking the bear came out of the bush and began heading toward my camp again. I yelled at him 'If you come over that log, that's as far as you'll ever come.'" The bear put its front paws on the log, lifted up its nose, sniffed noisily, and then turned around and left camp. Faille went back to his cooking. But two days later he shot a big black bear very similar to the one that had been hanging around his camp. "I don't know for sure if it was the same one, but it sure looked like it," he said.

The cheeky curiosity of wolverines infuriated Faille. He said they would steal anything they could carry. Whether they could eat it or not was immaterial. "There was a guy who came into the Nahanni once to hunt and he shot a moose," said Faille. "He skinned it, but it was too late to move the meat so he camped right there beside it. In the morning he woke up and his meat was okay but his gun was gone." An Indian told the hunter that a wolverine must have stolen the gun, but the man refused to believe such a tale. He was scared stiff and moved out. So the Indian circled the place where the man's camp had been and, sure enough, he found the rifle not far away, obviously dragged into the bush by a wolverine.

Faille's first encounter with wolves happened when he was living in a cabin beside a snye (a river channel or backwater) above Virginia Falls. "I was going hunting and I went to get into my canoe, but first I looked to see if there was any holes in it," said Faille. "Then my dogs started barking and I thought there must be something behind my shack. So I made a circle around the shack, but I didn't see no tracks in the snow, so I went back to the canoe. Then the dogs started barking again, so I made a bigger circle around the shack and still didn't see no tracks. I bawled out the dogs and told them if they didn't shut up, I would take a club to them. It was like they were saying to me 'you damn fool, there's something behind there.' "

Seconds later, Faille heard wolves howling down the river and immediately ran into his cabin and dumped a box of ammunition into his pocket. Well armed, he headed down the snye in the direction of the howling, but he still could not see any tracks. "I sat down then to have a smoke and as I was starting to fill my pipe they started to howl again," he said. "So I stuffed my pipe and tobacco back in my pocket and started through the bush to where the noise was. I got into the bush just a little ways and then another bunch of wolves started to howl right across from me. I stepped over a kind of ridge and there was an old snye in front of me and across the snye was a bunch of wolves that started to howl." Faille just kept on going and when he reached the frozen snye, the wolves began making a whinnying noise "just like a bunch of pups." Suddenly one of them came straight toward him.

"As the first wolf was coming toward me, another wolf came out on the snye, and then another one and another one. By that time the first wolf jumped up on top and I pulled the trigger, and I could see I had hit him in the right place. I leaped up and I had the wolves covered all the time. The wolf I'd shot went past me leaning over heavily, maybe two feet from my leg, and then he threw himself back and landed with his head only six inches from my foot. He was stone dead when he fell."

As for the rest of the pack, one stepped back into the bush as Faille took aim, and the others vanished like white streaks between the trees. "I thought I better get out of there, there was too many of them," he said.

The second time wolves nearly disposed of Faille was when he was lying in his camp, sick with scurvy. Patterson visited the camp in 1951, not long after Faille recovered, and said the place stank to high heaven because of the bodies of seven wolves lying around. "The wolves had come right up to his mosquito net when he was sick," said Patterson. "They sensed a sick animal, of course, and Albert shot them from where he lay."

Faille did not know he had scurvy until he bit into a piece of fresh bread one day and saw blood on it. "Scurvy works on you until you get weaker and weaker," he said. "But I was lucky, because I remembered Gus Kraus had planted some potatoes down at his cabin at the hot springs, and he hadn't dug them up when he left. So I went down to the springs with a pail and shovel and dug up a sixteen-quart pail full of potatoes. I ate nothing but potatoes for a week and began to get better. When I left the springs, I dug up some more and took them with me. Then I shot a sheep, and if you have enough fresh meat you never get scurvy — but you have to eat some of it raw."

Faille recovered from scurvy because he acted quickly and intelligently to cure himself, but the disease left him with loose teeth. He solved that problem by pulling out the wobbly ones with a pair of pliers. Later on, he developed a severe toothache and not even pliers would budge the rotten tooth. "I damn near went mad with the pain, so I made a pair of forceps out of a couple of traps," he said. "I tied a string to the forceps and started to pull, but that didn't work, because the string stretched. So then I tied on some wire instead of the string and I pulled and heard a crack— the tooth came out and the toothache vanished." A doctor removed most of his other teeth, but he still hung on to a few uppers of which he was very proud. "I went back to get the forceps from the cabin some time later, but someone had taken them," he said regretfully.

Very occasionally Faille became sick or had an accident, but he hated to talk about it. "I got tangled up a few times, but nothing serious," was all he would say. Turner said a war-time back injury of Faille's caused trouble several times. Once he aggravated the injury by falling on some ice and had to lie in bed in his cabin for a month. Another time he went blind for a short period, probably an effect of scurvy, and he gathered firewood by tying a rope to the cabin door and then roaming in the bush at the end of the rope. When he had picked up an armful of wood, he used the rope to guide himself back to the cabin. "But mostly you need good luck to live alone in the bush and Albert had it," said Patterson. "A very simple accident can kill you, but you become very careful with your feet and develop a very light step."

The most incredible part of Faille's long and solitary life in the Nahanni was his portage around Virginia Falls. Not once, but many times he trudged up this precipitous trail, carrying a boat, piece by piece, from the lower to the upper Nahanni River.

When Faille first started exploring the Nahanni he used a canoe but later switched to a flat-bottomed river boat, which he made himself out of lumber whipsawed on the river bank. He packed this boat up to the top of the falls in separate pieces.

Patterson saw the boat in 1960, when he paid a brief flying visit to Faille at his Fort Simpson cabin. "He showed me a pile of lumber outside his cabin and I said, 'That's a funny-looking boat,' " recalled Patterson. "Then Albert told me every piece was numbered and shaped." Faille explained that after packing the boat up the trail he put the pieces together at the top, carefully matching all the numbered and shaped boards.

The trail up the side of the 316-foot falls once had logs set in the clay and gravel, like a series of steps, put there by the Klondikers in the gold rush of 1898. One of the routes to the goldfields led up the Nahanni and across a mountain range to the Pelly River in the Yukon. Few of the miners who picked this route ever reached the Klondike, because the journey was a killer. Rain eventually washed away the log steps, but they were still there in 1927 when Faille and Patterson first saw the falls. The portage is one mile uphill and it took Faille a week of climbing up and down the rocky trail to pack all his belongings to the upper river. He climbed steadily, pulling himself up by the wild rose bushes which grow profusely in the Nahanni valley. He dragged each piece of lumber over his shoulder or tucked under his arm, and his outboard engine was hauled up inside an old canvas bag. At the top it was always time for tea—a strong brew sipped out of an enamel mug beside a glowing fire.

"The trail was so steep you almost rubbed your nose on the rock when you went up the cliff," said Faille. "It was good hard work. I had to get everything up there—boat, food, gasoline and traps." At the top of the falls he put his boat together and then explored upriver for about a month every year, but he never found the gold mine.

The feat was so amazing that in 1961 the National Film Board of Canada made a film about it. In that year Faille was seventy-three and the film "Nahanni" shows the bent, but still immensely strong, old man on his never-ending search for gold. "I will be dead or drowned before I quit," he told the cameraman. He was very proud of the film, but shrugged off his own performance. "The scenery's very nice but the old dog don't look so good," he snorted.

Although the gold was elusive, Faille had few complaints about the trapping in the Nahanni, which he did for years until 1952, when he was sixty-five. Then, even he admitted the winter trails were too tough for him. "Trapping is a young man's game," he said. "You could make it hard or you could make it easy—that's up to you. But if you want to make money trapping, you've got to work."

Dick Turner is probably the person who knows Faille best, because in 1954 he and his family moved their home and trading post to Nahanni Butte and started seeing a lot of the old man. Every summer, Faille would stop off for a few days at the Turners' on his annual trip to the country above the falls. And he would stop again on his way back, because by then he was spending his winters in Fort Simpson rather than the bush. He loved being fussed over by Turner's wife, Vera, who always baked a batch of cinnamon buns for him. "He figures Vera's a hundred per cent," said Turner. "He was very close to us in those years and we learned to love him. He's had no formal education and we soon realized that if we left a note for him, it should be written in capitals. But he's an amazingly good engineer, he just has a natural aptitude for it."

This close bond with Turner saved Faille's life in 1958, when he overturned his boat in First Canyon. Faille's disastrous trip started smoothly enough in July, when he made the 120-mile trip from Fort Simpson to Nahanni Butte with a boat load of about a hundred gallons of gasoline. He stopped off at the Turners' as usual and seemed as capable as ever of guiding his boat through the rocks and waves of his beloved river. "More than many we know, Albert loves the challenges of the river and the lonely places far from men," wrote Turner in his book. But in that year Faille was seventy and the challenge was almost too much for him.

"It was the wind that was the cause of it," Faille said. "I was right close to the bank in the First Canyon and a puff of wind came across, one of them twisters, you know, and shot me right up against the bank and the motor stopped as I hit the rocks." Faille quickly used the other outboard to steer himself out into the stream again, but "another puff of wind come along and drove me back onto the rocks." That killed his second motor. "So I grabbed my paddle to get the boat away from the rocks, but there was a big boulder out there and instead of sheering off the boulder, my boat went right up on it and tipped over," said Faille.

"The next thing I knew, I was under the boat, which was upside down. I don't know how long I was in the water. First, when I looked up, it was dark and the next time it was daylight." The boat began to drift downstream and Faille climbed on top of it and stayed there until the river swept around a sharp bend. "I didn't want to go around the bend with the boat, because I knew there were two bad places just below there," he said. "So when we got near the bank I jumped off, but the water was going too strong for me to swim. If I'd had a stick I could have stood up but I didn't so I crawled out on all fours." The boat vanished around the bend and Faille found himself ashore on a narrow shelf of rock and spruce trees, with the canyon walls rising up steeply behind.

"It started to cloud up and I was wet and cold," said Faille. "I had nothing left but what I had on, my jacknife, and a box of matches that was in my pocket. I'd lost my hat, of course." He had also lost two years' supply of food and his $400 savings wrapped up in foil in his grub box. "My watch was still ticking, so I opened it up and dried it," said Faille. "Then I spread out the matches on a rock to dry." He gathered some birch bark to make a fire, but had trouble with the wet matches. Out of twelve matches in the box he only managed to light three. When he finally lit a fire, he dried out and collected enough moss and wood to keep the blaze going all night.

"It rained all night, and next day I didn't want to try climbing out of the canyon, because rocks are slippery and dangerous when they are wet," he said. "I had to wait until four o'clock next afternoon before starting to climb out." It was a rugged climb, but he made it. Next he had to negotiate two smaller canyons and it took him three days to reach the hot springs.

"I didn't have any food because I'd lost it all in the boat and I hoped there'd be some berries at the hot springs," said Faille. "But the bears had been there before me so there were no berries." Four-and-a-half days had gone by since he had landed in the river and his matches were used up. To keep warm at night, he dug a hole under a big tree with a stick and buried himself in moss, pulling his jacket over his head. But luck was not with him. When he climbed down to the river from the hot springs, he took a shortcut and missed the place where his boat had lodged on a sandbar. Then a boat chugged down the river carrying the local forest warden and another man, but they didn't see him. However, the two men gave the alarm for Faille, after finding his overturned boat and a message he had left in the canyon, written in charcoal on birchbark, that he had swamped and would try to walk to Nahanni Butte.

Turner took up the story at this point. He was on his own at Fort Liard when an RCMP constable told him of Faille's accident. So Turner went into action on his own. He talked some geologists at Fort Liard into lending their helicopter for an air search. The weather was poor, but the pilot was game, so he and Turner took off in rain and fog, stopping only at the Butte to organize some Indians into a

Albert Faille
215

ground search of the river by canoe. "The country for the last thirty miles to the Butte is a mess of snyes, swamps, windfalls two feet high, tangled rose bushes and willows," said Turner. By now he was very worried about his old friend. The helicopter pilot touched down near Faille's overturned boat, but there were no footprints around. All day they searched, thinking that every wisp of fog was campfire smoke, but there was no sign of Faille. What they did not know was that he had left the river that day and walked to Jackfish Lake, where he thought there was a cabin. But he was mistaken about the cabin, and when he heard a plane in the distance he returned to the river.

"It rained that night and I went down to the river bank as soon as I got dried out a little," said Faille. "I decided to stay there until ten o'clock and, if nothing came along, I'd start to walk again. My shoes were full of water, so I took them off and wrung my socks out. I was wet right up to my hips from walking through the bush. I sat down for a while and then walked back and forth, back and forth."

Meanwhile, back in Fort Liard, Turner had talked the helicopter company into one more day of searching. The machine flew up the river following every bend and suddenly, pilot Bob Taylor spotted Faille on the beach. Taylor landed the helicopter on some slough grass and in seconds Turner ran the hundred yards through the bush to the river. He wrote in his book:

> I ran up the beach to meet Albert and grasped him by the hand. The truth is there were tears in my eyes. His hands were cold as ice and this was August 2nd. "Albert," I said, "how are you?" "Oh, I'm fine," he said, but his voice was very feeble and more squeaky than usual. "Where did you come from, Dick?" he asked. "The chopper," I said, "Didn't you hear the chopper?" "Yeah, I thought I heard an engine, but I didn't know it landed."

"The first thing he asked for was a piece of bread and butter and a cup of tea," said Mrs. Turner, who looked after the old man for the next two weeks, watching him regain his strength. "Albert's had quite a few experiences, but I think that was the most traumatic. He doesn't know when he's beat, I guess that's what saved him."

Faille was quite sure he could have walked the last thirty miles to the Butte, but Turner disagreed. "It was real jungle from where we found him to the Butte," he said. "I don't think he could have lived another two or three days." Someone retrieved Faille's boat and brought it back to the Butte for him and he spent the rest of the summer in Fort Simpson earning money at odd jobs.

Faille was not quite sure when he finally quit making his annual excursions up the Nahanni in search of the McLeod gold, but he was certainly well into his seventies before his boat was hauled out of the river for the last time. And even then he continued to search occasionally in Turner's plane. Faille shugged off all deaths in Headless Valley as accidents—"a bear, a wolf or a slide."

He was convinced that the McLeod brothers died of starvation and that animals made off with their skulls. "I had trouble finding food in the valley once myself," said Faille. "For a whole month from August tenth to September tenth, I didn't even see a rat. I knew there was game around, but it was up high and not in the valley. I figure that's what happened in Deadmen's Valley—the men didn't see no game and they stayed there until they starved to death."

And Faille just laughed at rumors of fierce Indian tribes, because in all his years in the valley he met only one Indian family, and these Indians were more superstitious than fierce. The father of the family would not let his dogs eat sheep meat because of some long-forgotten taboo. And killing a wolf was absolutely forbidden. "If a wolf got caught in his trap he'd just throw it away and not use the fur," said Faille, who thought that particular custom might have had something to do with the Indians' reincarnation beliefs.

"Before the white man came, the Indians just used to drink moose-milk, which is distilled rice," he said. "I could drink a pail of it and it wouldn't hurt me, but they drink it with imagination. After the white man came they drank things like fuel oil and they had stills to make whiskey, but they drink the booze like water and they can't take it."

What Faille really loathed in the Nahanni—apart from wolverines—were mosquitoes, but luckily they were never a permanent part of the scene. "Sometimes they were so goddamned thick you couldn't see for more than twenty-five yards and they drove you crazy," he said. "There was none of the dope you have nowadays to keep them off. We just used bacon rind and smoke from a fire to try to keep them away. The dogs go mad with mosquitoes and get so close to the fire they scorch themselves. My ears were sticking right out from bites and my hands were swelled up twice their normal size.

"I've known snow in the valley every month of the year and that keeps them away a lot of the time. I've known the ponds to freeze on August twenty-fourth. You might get ice in your water bucket any time of the year, and that's what keeps the mosquitoes down."

How did Faille manage to survive all the hazards of life in the Nahanni that killed so many other men? "Done the right thing, I guess," was his answer. Turner added his own ideas. "Water ability is the most amazing thing about Albert," he said. "He's like a Newfoundland dog—he likes nothing better than to be on the water. He has no fear of the water and I think that's why he's run it a little too close, taking careless chances now and again.

"He never cuts himself with an axe. He's always careful with guns, he's careful about food supplies. The only time he's come a cropper was when the river just about got him. He's had three or four terribly close accidents in the water, but he can swim and that saved his life."

Turner recalled watching Faille on his last few trips

up the Nahanni, when he was a thin and bent old man. "When he got into his boat it was all he could do to turn the kickers over, and when he got them going he'd turn to us and say goodbye, and a great smile of happiness and contentment came over his face—he just loved to be on the water again."

In retirement, Faille used to do all kinds of odd jobs around Fort Simpson—babysitting or setting out the chairs for a public meeting and sweeping the hall out afterward. "I did the jobs everyone else was too high and mighty to do," he said. As age and frailty advanced on him, he retreated to his cabin where his days became filled with mail and visitors. Sometimes the visitors split wood for him, brought some caribou meat, or checked on his health. Everyone in Fort Simpson kept an eye on Faille.

"He has no enemies," said Turner. "He's never done any harm to anyone and he's done a lot of good things for people."

Faille never found his gold mine, but he did spend his life exactly the way he pleased, which is something few men can say. Turner was sure that Faille enjoyed every minute of the years he spent battling the Nahanni, except for the few times when he was down for the count. He put it this way: "All things considered, I would say some rounds ended in a draw, but if a decision was to be awarded, I would vote it would go to Albert."